S.H.I.T–
Servicemen Have It Tough

S.H.I.T –
Servicemen Have It Tough

JAMES E. WIMES

Copyright © 2012 by James E. Wimes.

Library of Congress Control Number:		2012919232
ISBN:	Hardcover	978-1-4797-3261-6
	Softcover	978-1-4797-3260-9
	Ebook	978-1-4797-3262-3

All rights reserved. No part of this book may be reproduced or transmitted in any form or by any means, electronic or mechanical, including photocopying, recording, or by any information storage and retrieval system, without permission in writing from the copyright owner.

This book was printed in the United States of America.

To order additional copies of this book, contact:
Xlibris Corporation
1-888-795-4274
www.Xlibris.com
Orders@Xlibris.com
117781

Contents

Chapter 1:	The Start of a Career	11
Chapter 2:	The Induction Center	15
Chapter 3:	California or Bust	18
Chapter 4:	Philippine Islands	24
Chapter 5:	Sweet Home Alabama	29
Chapter 6:	Vietnam	32
Chapter 7:	The Sunshine State of Florida	39
Chapter 8:	Red Horse in Korea	43
Chapter 9:	Georgia on My Mind	48
Chapter 10:	The Philippines; Start of a Family	56
Chapter 11:	Return to the Sunshine State	78
Chapter 12:	Coco Clock and Brats	83
Chapter 13:	Defense Equal Opportunity Management Institute	88
Chapter 14:	The Family Pet	93
Chapter 15:	Back to the Land of Oz Once More	103
Chapter 16:	My Miracle Child	109
Chapter 17:	The End of SHIT	117

[DEDICATION]

This book is dedicated to the many men and women of the United States Armed Services, whether they are in the US Army, Navy, Air Force, Marines, or Coast Guard. As a fellow service person, I too applaud you for putting your life on the line to protect the American way of life. A standing ovation is in order for those service men and women, as well as their families that paid the ultimate price for our country. Without the thousands of military personnel that touched my life for almost a half century, this book could not have been written. This is simply my way of saying I too understand the essence of (SHIT) "Servicemen Have It Tough."

Preface

This book was penned to tell the life story of James Ellis Wimes, a United States Military Service personnel. The title of this book was derived as a marketing strategy. S H I T is eye-catching to the average American. For some reason, Americans have a fascination for profanity. I hope that once a person opens this book, he or she will realize that S H I T truly expresses why I feel that Servicemen Have It Tough. This book tells the story of my life from August 1962 to the present. Although I retired from active duty on February 22, 1989, you will see how my military career continues to impact me till date. This book tells the entire story of my life, loves, friends, and experiences spanning more than forty years. Some of the stories are funny, some are serious, some are sexy, but above all, they are true. So sit or lie back, and enjoy why joining the United States Military will create many situations of S H I T—Servicemen Have It Tough.

Chapter 1

The Start of a Career

In April 1962, I made a decision that was to have an impact on the rest of my life. I attended Peter G, Appling High School in Macon, Georgia, as I had done for almost four years. I was a senior, had an English IV exam, and knew that I was not prepared. Mr. James Harden was my favorite teacher, but he did not play when it came to his test. As fate would have it, the United States Air Force (USAF) recruiter (TSgt Harvey C. Joyner) was giving the USAF entrance exam. If I had gone to Mr. Harden's class and failed the English test,

I may not have graduated with my class of 1962. If I took the USAF exam and failed, it only meant that I would not be going to the air force. I had not planned on joining the military anyway, so I had nothing to lose. However, taking the air force exam was a great excuse for avoiding the language arts midterm exam.

I took the test. When the scores were released, I had passed with flying colors. However TSgt. Joyner started sweating me to join the USAF. He called almost every day, trying to get me to sign up. He was told to forget it because I was going to college at Tuskegee Institute in Alabama. I had already been accepted to this prestigious college, home of the famed Tuskegee Airmen of the 99th Pursuit Squadron of World War II.

My family wanted me to attend a college in Georgia such as Fort Valley State or Morehouse College. Being young and dumb, I saw Fort Valley State as a country school and Morehouse College as a boys school. The dumbness was me not realizing that the famous girls school, Spelman College, was directly across the street from Morehouse College. The one thing I did know was that all the boys I knew who attended Morehouse were very smart, such as Bryant Price, and the Nobel Peace Prize winner, Dr. Martin Luther King, Jr. Bryant was so smart that he skipped a grade in elementary school and graduated from Peter G Appling High School in three years. I, on the other hand, being a good "C" student had to beg Dr. Doris Adams to give me a "D" in French so I could graduate with my class.

I did graduate from Peter G. Appling High School and thus became the first member of my family to be awarded a high school diploma. That in itself was an honor for my family.

The summer of 1962 went on as usual, with me writing several letters to Tuskegee Institute trying to get a job and grants so I could start my first year. I also inquired about the USAF ROTC (Reserve Officers Training Corp). Cadets Harold Woodall, Edmond Leonard, and Carl Glover would return to Macon, Georgia, wearing their uniform with those beautiful burgundy sashes hanging down. I wanted that sash, but it was not to be.

There were many girls in my life during high school. Joyce Akridge, Joyce Jackson, Jacqueline Bradswell, Jacqueline Myles, Renilda Wilson, Pearlie Tolliver, and Gwendolyn Webb were all nice young ladies. However, it was Joyce Akridge that had my nose wide open. Each summer, Joyce would spend the summer in Chicago with her two sisters, Juanita and Virginia. The summer of sixty-two is the summer that started my "SHIT."

Phil, Larry Hicks, Benny Stephens and I were playing street football on Madison Street in the Pleasant Hill Section of Macon, Georgia. A neighbor of Joyce drove by and stopped for a conversation. He lived a few houses down the street from Joyce. He asked me if I had seen Joyce. My response was "Joyce is in Chicago." He said Joyce came home from ChiTown last Friday. I just knew he was lying because I had gone to her house that Friday afternoon. Her mother told me she had no idea when her daughter was coming home.

The neighbor convinced me to go and call Joyce. I went into Benny's house to make the call. To my surprise the voice on the other end of the line said, "Joyce speaking." I was so hurt because that day was Monday, August 22, 1962, and the most important person outside my family had not called to tell me she had returned from Chicago. I was hurt a second time when I asked if I may visit her She said "No, Jimmy is coming over." My name is James but she never called me Jimmy. I was through playing street football. As I walked up the street to my house, all I could do was cry. I was so distraught seeing Joyce was the only cure. She was indeed the love of my life.

Cutting school was a no-no in my Otha Mae's house. Whenever I would cut Peter G. Appling High School, a visit to Ballard-Hudson High School was in order, just to walk Joyce home. Those were fun memories but this had to be the worst day of my life. When I arrived home, I asked my mother if I could use the car to go visit Joyce. She said no because all I did was use up all the gas. At the time, gasoline was only fifteen cents per gallon, but in those days, my mother earned only $27.50 a week doing domestic work and raising two little white boys.

After Momma refused to let me use the car, I decided that I had to get out of Macon, Georgia. You know how a person can make a comment under their breath to their parents. I said, "I am going to leave here." My mother heard me and responded with, "You have been leaving for eighteen years." That was all it took. I went into the living room and got on the telephone. The call was to TSgt. Joyner. I told him that I was ready to join the USAF. He said, "But I thought you were going to college?" I informed him that things have changed, and I wanted to join the military. He said that he had a group leaving in two weeks. Then I told him, "That is too long to wait." He then said there were some recruits leaving in the morning, August 23, 1962. I said, "That would be great." By that time, the sergeant had become suspicious and wanted to know if I was in any kind of trouble. He asked if I'd mind if he checked with the city police.

He called back in less than twenty minutes. He said if I was serious, he would go to his office right then and prepare my paperwork, which I could pick up the next day along with bus tickets to Atlanta. It was a safe bet that TSgt Joyner had not met his quota of enlistees for the month of August, 1962, proving that even recruiters are subject to SHIT.

The morning of August 23, 1962, I got up early and started packing my few clothes in a brown paper bag. My mother, Otha Mae, thought I was lying about leaving. I asked if she and my stepfather, Willie Deshazer, could drive me to the post office to pick up my enlistment papers. Once I returned to the car with a big stack of papers, Mother started crying. She continued to cry until we arrived at Joyce's house. I went into her house to bid her good-bye, and to let her know how much she meant to me, and how much she had hurt me. After a few precious moments with Joyce, I returned to our 1954 ford, for a ride to the Greyhound bus station to begin my life of SHIT.

CHAPTER 2

The Induction Center

My trip to Atlanta, Georgia, took about three hours. I was becoming concerned; in fact, I was now a little scared. This was the first time in my life I was leaving the nest. I was traveling alone. When I arrived at the bus station in Atlanta, there were two sharp military men to greet me. Their job was to meet all recruits and load them onto buses for a short trip to Fort McPherson, Georgia. Fort Mack, as it is called, is the induction center for all branches of the military. It is at Fort Mack that every military member takes their medical exams. If you pass the medical and physical exam, you are then placed in this gigantic room with thousands of other men who had volunteered for the US Navy, Army, Air Force, and Marines. Then there were those men that were drafted by the selective services system who would be going into the US Army. This was important due to the Vietnam War that was in full swing thus proving that one does not have to volunteer to be victim of SHIT.

Around 1600 hours, all recruits took the oath of enlistment and were sworn into the United States Military. At 1700 hours we were brought to the position of attention for transportation to the various military boot camps. It was during that hour, I realized that I was special and was smarter than what I had given myself credit for. The officers and NCOs (Non-Commissioned Officers) began with verbal orders, "All recruits that will be taking the buses to Fort Jackson Army Military Training Center, stand in a single file and march out. All recruits that will be taking the Delta Flight to San Diego Naval Military Training Center, stand in a single file and march out." In both cases, a very large number of the new military personnel left the large room. As I looked around, there were still a large number of recruits left to go with me to Texas. Boy! Was I wrong! When the sergeant said, "All recruits that will be taking the Continental flight to San Antonio, Texas, Lackland Air Force Basic Military Training Center stand in a single file and march out," I jumped up and was the only one of the three inducted into the USAF. By the way, the other two recruits were Caucasian. I was still alone. The service personnel left in the large room would be taking the buses to South Carolina, Parris Island, Marine Basic Military Training Center.

My flight from Atlanta to San Antonio was very exciting because it was my first airplane ride. It was also the first part of my dream coming true. In a few hours I would be getting my USAF blue uniform. I arrived at Lackland AFB, Texas, about 2300 hours from the airport.

There were about fifty of us. There were three recruits from Georgia and forty-seven from the New York area. Can you imagine a black and two white men trying to defend the south. My training instructors were TSgt (Technical Sergeant) Jack and A1C (Airman First Class) Palmer. These two men were like Dr. Jekyll and Mr. Hyde. From the very first minute, I knew I had made a great mistake.

TSgt. Jack marched the flight to the mess hall for breakfast. It was the first and last time I was fed cream beef on toast, better known in the military as S O S (Shit on a Shingle). That was the worst food I have ever eaten. S O S makes chitterlings taste like French pastries. August 23, 1962, was a long day, so I was ready for bed when we were told to do so around 0130 hours.

At 0500 hours, A1C Palmer awakened the barrack by turning on the lights and shouting, "Get your lazy asses out of those racks. You have five minutes to use the latrine, get dressed in those nasty clothes you wore here, and fall in outside." For the first time in my life, I was placed on the same level with everyone else. We were referred to as the rainbow flight because of the multicolored clothing we wore. Our first order of business was to get a haircut. The barbers had an easy job because we were all given a close haircut. Our heads were shaved to the scalp. We looked like a group of cabbage heads rolling down the street. The shaved heads was the USAF's method of making us all equal and ready for training into a life of SHIT.

San Antonio, Texas, feels like the hottest place in the world during the month of August and September. During boot camp, there were many days I prayed for that almighty red flag to be raised. The raising of the red flag signified that it was too hot for outside activities. The cabbage heads would be marched to early lunch or dinner. From the mess hall we were taken to the barrack. The red flag would get you out of the heat but not out of work. During red flag time we had to clean, polish, and spit-shine hats, shoes, floors, and toilets. To be caught sitting on your bed during red flag time was an automatic K. P. (kitchen police) duty washing pots and/or peeling potatoes. Nobody wanted KP duty. It would be like getting out of the Texas heat and into a Texas frying pan.

Boot camp was hard but only because of the temperature. The food in basic training was great with the exception of the cream beef. I went to basic training weighing 128 lbs. I finished up weighing 144 lbs. in perfect physical condition. The one highlight of basic training was going to a high school football game at Breckenridge Park in downtown San Antonio. At that game, I met a young lady by the name of Jeanette Rabb. Jeanette was so pretty that Joyce Akridge was put in the back seat. I thought I had met the girl of my dreams. She and I talked on the phone almost daily. Jeanette and I went out several times over the last four weeks of my training. On one date, we went back to the place where we first met, for lunch. Jeanette ordered a plate of rattle snake and French Fries. Being the macho man that I am, I decided to order the same dish. If she could eat rattle snake, so could I. However, when I put that snake in my mouth it appeared to have swollen ten times its size. I was so embarrassed when I began to throw up all over the table. Jeanette and I continued to talk on the phone many times after the rattle snake experience, but we never went out again. Graduation day was exciting because I was now a full member of the USAF. I departed Lackland AFB for Macon, GA, and my beloved Joyce Akridge.

Chapter 3

California or Bust

I flew to Atlanta from Texas and took a bus to Macon. I could not wait to get home to my family and friends. I also wanted to show off my new uniform. After greeting the family, a call to Joyce was in order. Her mother told me she had gone to Ballard-Hudson HS's football game. My stepfather drove me to Porter Stadium. Naturally, I wore that beautiful USAF blue uniform of which I was so proud. I found Joyce, and my homecoming was fulfilled. She and I renewed our relationship. We spend the next fifteen days making up for the summer and the time in Texas.

My request was to be assigned anywhere east of the Mississippi River. Instead, my first assignment was two-thousand miles west of the mighty river. The USAF gave me the second taste of SHIT.

S.H.I.T—Servicemen Have It Tough

Being a country boy from Georgia, traveling outside the state was not an option, so I decided to take the Grey Hound bus to my new assignment in California. The reason for taking the bus was so I could sightsee, from Macon, GA to Merced, California, home of Castle Air Force Base. Little did I know that the majority of sights to be seen were passed at night. My first encounter with the real world was just ninety miles from home in Atlanta, the first leg of my trip.

I had saved $25 for food and sodas on the three-day trip to the west coast. As I stood at the bus station, I was confronted by a slick hustler. He showed me a way I could double my money. He first let me win five dollars then another five dollars. I was on a roll. The young man then asked me to raise the stakes. Me being green as a pool table and twice as square said, "Sure!" After all, I had taken him for ten dollars. He said, "Let's play for $15.". In less than one minute, I had lost the ten I thought I had won, plus $20.00 of my food and soda money. Now with only $5 left, I could not play anymore. For the next three days, I would be on a bus and would have to eat. Fortunately for me, my dear sweet mother had made a shoebox filled with southern-fried chicken, light bread, and slices of pound cake for me. For three days, I ate very little and drank a lot of water while traveling to California. Atlanta also gave me the opportunity to meet a nice young lady with her three sons. She was going to Los Angeles to meet her husband. For three days, she held her baby, and the other two boys were forever on me. We finally reached Los Angeles. The lady and the boys were met by a nice gentleman they called Daddy. After three days and nights with those boys, I was happier to see the daddy than they were.

A totally new arena opened for me in Los Angeles. I had spent the last three days and nights on a bus. Sometimes I was hungry and always tired due to those two boys from Georgia. I could not wait for the last leg of my trip.

While waiting to hear the announcement of the north-bound bus; I heard this beautiful female voice. "Hello there, you in the blue uniform." I immediately started looking for the owner of the voice and the other blue uniform. Not finding either, I sat back savoring my solitude. Again this soft but seductive voice said, "Yes, I am talking to you in the air force-blue uniform." I looked up in time to catch the ugliest man in the world hitting on me. Hello California! I told that mentally challenged fool that I was tired and hungry. Sex with a beautiful woman was the farthest thing from mind, forget a nasty, ugly-ass gay man. All I could do was to call him a few MF's and a couple of SOB's. Again is this California, or is this more SHIT?

This time the voice was through the loud speaker announcing that the northbound bus was now loading. Many cities north were called out and finally he said, "Merced." In less than ten hours, this sightseeing trip would be over. Castle Air Force Base, home of the 93rd Bombardment Wing is my first permanent assignment. When I first enlisted, I requested the AFSC (Air Force Specialty Code) for security police. Those young men were so sharp in their slick uniforms, directing traffic and giving information to visitors. The USAF decided that I could best serve my country as a carpenter. I was given an AFSC of 55210, an apprentice woodworking specialist. This job meant fixing leaky roofs four days in a week and cleaning the shop on Fridays. Just imagine cleaning a woodshop full of dust and then studying my CDC's (Career Development Course). As I stumbled through training, my dislike for trees grew larger than the giant sequoias themselves.

Remember, I wanted to be a security police. Well as fate would have it, my luck finally hit the jackpot. The Military Police Unit ran short of personnel. Volunteers were requested to go on TDY (Temporary Duty) status to the security police unit. I quickly filed my application and was accepted along with about twenty other troop members. We were given a quick orientation on the duties. We were issued special equipment such as wet weather gear and an M-1 rifle. Each time I went to work, I was greeted by a B-52 Bomber or a KC—135 Tanker airplane. The planes needed a human being with a poncho and a rifle to walk around them for eight hours to ensure their protection. There were times when I would count the rivets to break the boredom. My tenure in the Military Police Unit was short-lived. As I got settled into counting rivets on planes, another note came from the base commander, requesting more volunteers. This time the USAF needed airmen to take a bypass test to become a telephone and teletype operator. It didn't take long for me to accept this invitation. After all, I could read and speak well. As a telephone operator, I would be working in an air conditioned or centrally heated environment. Also, I could make phone calls from California to the rest of the world. Moreover, I could call my mother and Joyce whenever I sat on the switch board. All calls were given priority numbers. The Operator used what was known as an OP (operator's personal). As a telephone operator, the amazing thing was my ability to remember over 90 percent of all telephone numbers on base.

The operator's gig lasted for six months. That was long enough to establish a wide array of female friends. One of the young ladies was the nice little white daughter of the vice-commander of the base. She would call me daily and before long we started having lunch together. One day, I was talking to her while I was on the switchboard when Lorraine, the chief operator, plugged into the line. She told the young lady not to call the switchboard except for business. The truth is that she had seen the nice, young, white girl pick me up for lunch. I told her to get off the damn line or I would kick her prejudiced ass. She left the switchboard went directly to the typewriter to log in my profanity and threat. The next day, I was ordered by Chief Master Sergeant, (CMSgt), Ben Little, to report to his office. He said Lorraine had written me up for profanity on the switchboard. I quickly said, "Yes, I meant every damn word." I have told you already that Lorraine was a racist. CMSgt. Little immediately dismissed me from communication and the 29130 AFSC. He sent me back to the black tar and the wood dust in the carpentry shop.

Don't forget, I met several other girls during my operator days. Particularly two black girls I met over the phone, one was Sue Kellebrew and the other was Sylvia Shellings. They were daughters of military service members. We talked when they were not in school at Atwater High School. Sue's nickname was run-around-Sue because of her many suitors. I didn't have any possible chance with Miss Kellebrew. Sylvia on the other hand enjoyed my company. Her family was also fond of me. Sylvia's father was a Technical Sergeant (TSgt) in the base supply unit. I thought he was the biggest, blackest, and meanest man in the USAF. He didn't want his two daughters dating anyone from Castle AFB. Sylvia on the other hand was crazy about Airman Wimes. She was a senior at Atwater High School and chose me as her prom escort. This prom date became a controversy. I was chosen in January, 1963, and by June 1963, Sylvia had been dating my friend Nathan Hill. Sylvia told Hill "Wimes is my date for the prom, and that's that." Hill now understands the full idea of SHIT.

Sylvia and I made a beautiful couple at the prom. She wore a light-blue evening gown. I was decked out in a black tux with white accessories. Our transportation was a white, 1960, convertible Impala with red interiors. We had a great time at the prom. After the prom, we went to dinner. The prom was uneventful but dinner was a different story. Neither Sylvia nor I were accustomed to fine dining. The waiter served us bread and water for starters. The funny thing was that we were buttering our bread with sour cream and wondered about the strange-tasting butter.

By the start of my second year in the air force, I had gained many friends. My best friend was Lafayette Mims. We were called the twins because of the pronunciation of our names, "Wims and Mims." We looked like Mutt and Jeff. Mims was only about 5'4" and I was six'. We once bought a car together, so we could go to Dad's Point Recreation Park in Stockton, California. It was at the park that Mims met his wife Connie, and I met Doris Jayvine, a friend of Connie's from Meridian, Mississippi. She became my girlfriend for that summer in 1964. Mims and I drove to Stockton almost daily and every weekend. Sometimes we slept in the car and when we had extra funds, even $5, we stayed at the YMCA. The summer ended and Doris returned to Mississippi. Several weeks passed, and I finally met a new girl at the park. Her name was Shirley Ivery. Shirley was the daughter of a Baptist preacher. She and I developed a serious relationship. We even entertained thoughts of marriage but as fate would have it, we split up. One Sunday, Shirley and I decided not to attend church with the family. We stayed home and had safe sex. I know it was safe because when her sister returned home, she found the condom floating in the pool. Her sister raised holy hell. I was order out their house. Shirley was sent to Los Angeles to live with her aunt. All I could say was SHIT.

Los Angeles was more than 300 miles from Castle AFB. Whatever the distance, I had to see Shirley. I agreed to do all the driving in order to get my friend, Sgt. Edward Smith, to make the trip with me. He loved the idea of me driving because he could stop at every wine tasting facility from Merced to LA When Smitty and I reached the Grapevine (a section of Interstate 99), south of Bakersfield, California, he was drunk as a skunk for free. I didn't have clue as to where I was going nor the danger of driving in the Grapevine at night. The road was very crooked with steep gradients. Some of the gradients served as a run-off for the big trucks when brakes created a problem.

We finally emerged from the worst highway I had ever traveled in my life. I was excited and after regaining my composure awakened Smitty. He raised his head long enough to tell me that we had another sixty miles to reach the City of Angels. He went back to sleep off his wine-tasting stops. Finally, I saw the sign giving me the directions to Crenshaw and Western Blvd. You can't imagine how happy I was to relinquish that Chevy Impala. We called a friend of ours who lived in LA, and he gave Smitty the directions to his house. I stopped at Sugg's house. Smitty went to visit his girlfriend.

The next morning I called Shirley Ivery to let her know that I was in Los Angeles. She didn't sound too thrilled to hear from me. We talked, and the more we talked, the more I knew she was not pleased about my visit to LA. She finally agreed to see me at Sugg's house in the afternoon. When she arrived, she told me she only came to tell me that I need not call, visit, or even write to her ever again which means I was a SHIT.

Needless to say, I was hurt and sick to my stomach. Sugg knew something was wrong when his mother announced that lunch was ready and I couldn't eat. The afternoon turned into night when Sugg felt my pain. He came to me and said, "I don't have a Shirley Ivery but I do have a Shirley Ing." She was called and invited to the party.

It was at this point that my Georgia country-ness came forth. Sugg informed me that Miss Ing would be at the "pot" party, later that night. I felt much better knowing I had a date for the "pot" party. Everyone started arriving for the pot party. I noticed that the vast majority of the attendees were smoking some stinking cigarettes. Being a non-smoker and having not eaten, I got hungry.

I found Sugg and asked what turned out to be the dumbest request of my life. I asked Sugg, "Where are the pots with the food?" He looked at me burst out laughing. He laughed so hard that he started crying. I thought we were at a "potluck party" where everyone attending brings a pot of food. When Sugg stopped laughing, he called me the dumbest ass country man he has ever met. How was I to know that "pot" was what potheads called marijuana. I was living proof of SHIT.

The Labor Day weekend ended. Smitty and I bade everyone farewell. He took the wheel for the drive back to Merced and Castle AFB. When we reached the Grapevine during daylight hours, I saw the dangers I had driven through three days earlier. Again, I was scared to death. It would be a year before I returned to the Los Angeles area.

Basketball in the military is an important sport because of which members of the team are allowed to travel throughout the country. I was never an outstanding basketball player. However, I was good enough to make the traveling squad. On one trip to the Bay Area, we were to play Oakland Army Post. We drove up the evening before so we could have some time to tour the city. Well, being the only twenty-year-old, I was the designated driver. After we settled into our billets, we loaded the van and headed to downtown Oakland and the Sportsman Club. Yes, I was too young, but back in the day, fake ids were not scrutinized as closely as they are today. While in the club, I met this fine, sexy woman who loved everything I had to say. I told the team captain Vernon Flowers that I was leaving for a few minutes with the van. Of course, he wanted to know where I was going and with whom. I pointed out the young lady at the bar. He went to take a closer look and came back laughing. Flowers said, "Son that lady's penis is much bigger than yours." After that incident, I had to have a CC and Ginger to help me deal with the SHIT.

Chapter 4

Philippine Islands

During the early fall of 1964, I was summoned to the orderly room (administration office). When I arrived there, the First Sergeant told me that I had received orders to be transferred to APO 96274. My first question was, "where in the hell is APO 96274?" "Clark Air Base, Philippine Islands," was his joyous response. I was not impressed. By then, I had had enough of the USAF. All I wanted to do was my next thirteen-month, and go home to Georgia, and my beloved Joyce Akridge.

In order to take the assignment I would have to extend my enlistment by five months because the overseas tour to the Philippines was eighteen months. I talked to several of my friends, all of whom were wishing they were in my shoes.

Even my best friend Smitty offered me fifty dollars to turn down the assignment because he was next in line for movement. Fifty dollars may not seem like a lot of money but remember SHIT. I only earned $ 152 a month as an A2C (Airman Second Class). If he was willing to pay that kind of money, then maybe I needed to rethink my decision. I extended my enlistment and received the reporting date of April, 1965. I could not wait to call home to tell Mom and Joyce. Neither one was pleased which I will get into later. Remember Sylvia Shelton, my first real prom date. Well, she and I kept in touch over the years, which meant I had to take one more trip to Los Angeles. This time, I was going to see a good friend. Sylvia's father had retired and moved to Compton, California. After all, she was my very first friend in California. In March, 1965, I went to Compton to visit the Shelton family. That was a wonderful visit with old friends. We hung out for the weekend and when it was over, Sylvia and I exchanged souvenirs. She gave me a silver dollar she had had since a baby, and I gave her my high school class ring. That was the last time I talked to my friend as I remembered SHIT.

I flew home taking a military hop to Robins AFB, Georgia, which is twenty-five miles south of Macon. A military hop is a free ride on a military aircraft to wherever the aircraft was going. Usually a service a male or a female could get for a couple hundred miles of their destination or as in my case twenty-five miles from home. My first visit was to Joyce. She told me she didn't want me to go to the Philippines. It was not until I got to Clark Air Base that I discovered the true reason as to why Joyce did not want me to accept the assignment. My first night in the PI was spent at the Coconut Grove Airmen's Club. It was at the club that I met a high school class mate, A1C Richard Douglas. Richard and I talked through the night about home, family, and friends.

Richard is by far the coolest man I know. He maintained his calmness as I bragged about my girlfriend, Joyce Akridge. When the night of homeboys' fellowshipping ended, Richard invited me to his barrack the next day. As soon as I arrived, he greeted me and threw open his wall locker. What do I see! To my surprise there was an 8×10 glossy photo of the love of my life, Joyce. She had been sending Richard the exact same things that she had been sending me. She once sent us both a copy of "The Sonnets from the Portuguese" by Elizabeth Barrett Browning, not to mention the letters which were the same word for word. Richard and I kept Joyce's behavior a secret for over a year. We wrote letters to Joyce pretending we did not know that she was playing two friends and fellow servicemen for fools. After a while, Richard could not take it anymore and wrote to her. He told her that he and I did not have to take caribou manure anymore. The military was bad enough without her adding to the SHIT.

The airmen's club was the place for fun and frolic. A live band played every night. There were more than a hundred Pilipino girls to dance with, talk with, and have dinner with. The Coconut Grove Airmen's Club was like any expensive American country club. It contained restaurants, barber shops, liquor stores, slot rooms, and pool and card rooms. On my third night at the club, I met who I thought was the most beautiful woman in the world, Amilita Patacog. I paid my dollar and chose Amilita. We talked and danced until I realized that Amy was not comfortable talking to me. That was her first night at work in the Coconut Grove Club. The evening with Amy ended early.

The next day, I arrived at the club and went directly over to speak to Amy. She began questioning me angrily as to why I had checked her out if I did not want to be with her. She went on to say, "I don't like black men anyway." When this beautiful woman attacked my race, she lost her charm where I was concerned. My fangs came forth. I told her to "kiss my black ass."

Amy quickly tried to defend her statement. She went on to explain that she had never talked to a black man in her life before. At that point, I felt sorry for Amy. She had been working in a white club off base. Even in the Philippines, segregation of blacks and whites was alive and working in 1965. In Angeles City, the Albacan Bridge separated the blacks and whites. There were Filipinos who aspired to be black and there were some that aspired to be white. However, when they decided to work on base where the commander was a black three-star General by the name of General Benjamin O. Davis, Jr. of the famed Tuskegee Airmen, their black and white feelings had to be left at the main gate of Clark Air Base. From that night on, I spent a dollar to check Amy out for an evening of chatting, dining, and dancing.

As time passed, she and I got very close. One night, she decided that she wanted to spend quality time with me. I borrowed my friend's car so I could take her home after she got off work at midnight. I could only pick her up at the main gate. Another Pilipino female friend, Gloria Pistilose or Big Glo, made arrangements for Amy and me to spend the night at her house.

Big Glo lived in a small one-bedroom house with one bed. Gloria liked me so much as a friend that she slept on the floor and gave us her bed. We spent many nights and days together for the rest of my tour. Amy told me later that she brushed her teeth for hours the next day to erase the thought of having kissed a black man. The one thing I knew was that our first night had been very good because it lasted for the rest of my tour. To make a long story short, Amy and I lived together for the rest of my tour.

Amy was ashamed to be seen with me because I was black. However, after living together, she finally got over the color of my skin especially after she realized that Michelle, her daughter, was the love of my life. I would give her money for herself and spend a large portion of the remaining funds on her daughter Michelle's health. Michelle was an eight-month blonde, blue-eyed soul sister. I fell in love with that little girl and would have given everything I owned to keep that baby healthy. Michelle became my daughter. Amy became the love of my life and possibly the future Mrs. James Wimes.

I was living at Amy's house; I stilled maintained a bed in the barrack. One day, while visiting my bed, I found a young man, Sandy Thomas, was preparing to get into my bed. Sandy said the First Sergeant had given him permission to use the bed because the owner was "shacking up" downtown. I went to see the First Shirt, as we called him, about the bed. He said, "Airman if you want that bed you damn well better sleep in it because I know you are living off base illegally." As for the bed, Sandy and I are still the best of friends and all there is to say about the bed is SHIT.

At this point, let's digress back to my first payday in PI I went to the orderly room to get my check. The First Sergeant gave me the check and then asked me to give it back saying, "Where you are going, you will not have a need for a check." He told me to report to the base terminal for deployment. Being a good airman, I followed his orders and reported to the terminal.

The clerk asked for my written orders otherwise he said I couldn't board the plane. That was fine with me, but a full colonel, James Baxter, overheard the exchange of words between the flight clerk and me. The colonel looked at the airman behind me and requested a copy of his flight orders. Colonel Baxter took the orders and wrote in large letters "VOCO—verbal orders of commanding officer—and my name beside it. Two-and-a-half hours later, we were landed at Mactan Air Strip, Mactan Island, Republic of the Philippines. The mission of the team was to repair and reopen the air strip as a C-130 Hercules aircraft refueling and staging base. The aircrafts were cargo planes bound for Vietnam loaded with supplies. From that point on, I became a member of an elite group of Civil Engineering personnel known as Prime Beef—Base emergency engineering force. The entire team expressed the sentiment that deployments like this were an example of prime SHIT.

I truly enjoyed the PI I had fallen in love with Amy and wanted to marry her. This caused me to drop the extension and I re-enlisted. The marriage was not to be because the promise of an extended tour at Clark Air Base was not granted. In fact the original tour was cut short due to temporary duty to

Southeast Asia. Ironically, the paper work allowing marriage to Amy came back with approval two weeks after I departed for a stateside assignment.

I also enjoyed the idea of buying clothes. As a young man in Macon, I was raggedy as a church mouse. I prayed to God to give me the means to buy clothes. My prayers were answered. I bought a suit almost every payday from my tailor and friend at Efren Tailors. His tailor shop was on the first floor of the apartment where Amy and I lived. When I returned to the good old USA, I shipped home around sixty suits, not to mention other apparel. Clothes were so cheap that a person could develop an addiction forbuying clothes. For instance, a three-piece-suit could be purchased for around fifty dollars. Efren was so good at his craft that I could call him from Thailand and he would have a new suit waiting for my return.

Once my little sister Sandra sent me a picture of a dress she wanted made. This dress was to be worn to her senior prom. I received the picture on Wednesday ten days prior to the prom. The only information was the picture and her measurements. Efren was given the task of making this dress in three days. I figured it would take me at least a week to get the dress from Clark Air Base to Macon, Georgia. Mr. Efren finished the beautiful blue dress on Sunday. The prom was the following Friday, five days and half a world away. I picked up the dress and placed it in a box, wrapped it in brown paper. Five dollars in US stamps were put on the package.

I then went to the base air terminal to find a person going to the southeast part of the United States. I found a gentleman going to Jacksonville, Florida. I explained my dilemma to him, and he agreed to take the package and mail it the minute he got home. To make this long story short, Sandra got the dress on Wednesday afternoon. My tailor was so good at his profession that all my sister had to do was to take the dress to the dry cleaners for ironing. She said that she felt like she was the belle of the ball because she wore a dress imported from the Philippine Islands.

Needless to say, I truly enjoyed the Philippine Islands. I had forgotten about Joyce and had fallen in love with Amy and her baby, Michelle. In fact, I dropped my enlistment extension and re-enlisted for another four years. My plan was to marry Amy and take them both back to the good old USA. This was not to be. Not only did the air force deny my tour extension, they cut my original tour short because I spent two months in Southeast Asia. It was a widespread belief that our government frowned on Americans marrying foreigners in the sixties due in part to the red scare of communism. My marriage to Amy was put on hold. Well, my clothes buying days finally came to an end when my extension request was denied and I received orders for Maxwell AFB, Alabama, or as they say, Sweet Home Alabama. The USAF had served me a healthy dose of SHIT.

Chapter 5

Sweet Home Alabama

Maxwell AFB, Alabama was my next sweet home. I took a thirty-day leave (vacation) in Macon before reporting. Joyce Akridge had moved to Chicago and besides Amy had written her a letter with all the particulars of our relationship. Needless to say, Joyce didn't want to see me. To my surprise, my adopted family had acquired a new boarder named Inez Gamble from Mobile, Alabama, who was a graduate from Alabama State College (ASC) in Montgomery. She came to Macon to teach math. Nettie Appling, my adopted sister, had built me up as her big brother, even though she was two years my senior. Inez and I were a hit right away. In fact, Inez became the new girl of my dreams. She and I dated heavily for three months.

She did warn me about the girls at ASC. Inez told me about many young ladies, but especially one by the name of Queen Walters. My first visit to ASC was exciting. However, the first person I met was Queen Walters. As soon as I told her I knew Inez Gamble, She was determined to get between Inez and me. Being a gentleman, I was determined to get between her legs. The best thing that happened to me was volunteering for Vietnam when I processed into Maxwell, AFB. The volunteer statement was accepted so fast that I did not have time to draw a paycheck. All in all, I spent thirty days leave before going to Maxwell, twenty-three days at Maxwell and thirty days leave departing from the Alabama base.

During my short stay in Alabama, I had a lot of time to meet several civilian females. Each night when I was not on campus, I was at Club Layco, downtown Montgomery. Those sixty suits I shipped home made me the best-dressed man in Alabama. I really stood out wearing a different suit each night. After about a week of clubbing, I had been talking hot and heavy to this superfine married lady. She admired my clothes. She finally agreed to let me take her out.

During my last week at Maxwell, AFB, we decided to visit Albert Picks Hotel. For those few days, I forgot about Inez in Macon, Georgia. I was thinking with the small head. That Wednesday was the highlight of my stay in Alabama. I checked into the hotel first and an hour later Dorothy arrived. She looked as fine as ever with her high, bright, and almost-white skin and long hair blowing in the wind. We immediately got down to business. I had my raincoat (prophylactic) beside the bed. Knowing she was a married woman, I assumed she would want me to use protection. I inquired about it and she said "You don't need that. I can't get pregnant." I was happy with her response. We had a ball that night.

That Thursday morning, Francis went home, and I went to the base to complete the processing for deployment to 37th Civil Engineering Squadron, Phu Cat Air Base, South Vietnam.

Everything went well during out-processing until I had to urinate. It was then that I noticed that my penis was glued to my drawers. At that point all I could think of was Inez. I went to the base hospital to pick up my medical records. However, due to a drip the size of Niagara Falls, I needed to see a doctor. Being a little embarrassed, I requested a male corpsman to a female nurse with the rank of major. The major quickly said, "Pull it out airman, I've seen one before." She smiled and took out a specimen slide which she pressed against the eye of my penis. She then left the room. About thirty minutes later, the major returned and directed me to report to a Master Sergeant in the public health office. If you know anything about the military at all, then you will know that sexually transmitted diseases are taken very seriously.

When I arrived at public health department, I was greeted by Master Sergeant Pillsbury Dough Boy. He started with the usual spiel of, "You need to save your fellow airmen by disclosing the source of your contact." My response was, "Sarge, just ask the questions, I'll tell you whatever you want to know about that filthy woman." I just could not believe that I had sex with hookers in the Philippines, Thailand, and South Korea without getting even the crabs (body lice), only to come home and get the clap from a married black woman. Needless to say, I was pissed off. I told the Pillsbury Dough Boy everything but Francis' mother's maiden name.

Being a gentleman, I called Francis to give her a heads up. I told her to go have herself checked out by a doctor because she could be sick. She got all indignant with me and started shouting that she had not given me any kind of STD, not to mention gonococcus. Still being a gentleman, I said, "Well, if you didn't give it to me, I have given it to you because I got it." I added, "By the way, did you make love to your husband last night because if you did, he's got the clap as well as you and me."

I left Maxwell, AFB, after receiving a healthy dose of penicillin from the largest syringe in the world that they used directly on my hip. I worried from Montgomery to Macon as to how was I going to explain to Inez that we could not make love. I even prayed to the man in the upper room for help. I decided to spend more time with my friends and so arrived home around 2300 hours. I immediately called Inez. In a matter of three hours, my prayers had been answered. Inez told me I could visit, but we could not make love because of her monthly period that came on three hours earlier. I wanted to say, "So did mine." I just looked and said, "Thank You, Dear Lord, for helping me out of this SHIT."

CHAPTER 6

Vietnam

Well, my vacation was great. Inez and I even talked of marriage after my tour in Vietnam. We didn't have a care in the world. In 1966, I was going to be home for Christmas and New Year's Day. We had plans to visit her family in Mobile. The military has a way of screwing up a wet dream. On December 15, 1966, I received a Western Union message from Headquarters USAF saying my leave had been cancelled and that I was to report to Travis AFB, California, on December 21, 1966, for a flight to Saigon, South Vietnam, on Flying Tiger Airline.

My plans for Christmas were over. I told Inez about the new orders that I'd received. She was very disappointed, but she understood. When I volunteered for Vietnam, I never expected my application to be accepted so fast. However, inspite of half a million personnel already there, replacements were badly needed. Plus, there were many servicemen wanting to be home by Christmas or at least by New Year's Eve. My change of orders made at least one person and one family happy. This is the positive side of SHIT.

As life would have it, the day before I was to depart for Vietnam, a city bus came over the hill on Madison Street and destroyed my 1962, Ford Galaxie. Most people would have been highly upset. To me the accident was a blessing in disguise. I had not made plans for my car and the insurance would have expired in three weeks. But the bus hitting a parked car in the middle of the day, it was a slam dunk case.

When I got to the bus station, I also got a lot of sympathy points. I showed the day shift supervisor my orders to Vietnam. He then made two calls to ford dealerships and got estimates to replace my car. After which he authorized a check for the amount of $1500 Boy! That was the SHIT. When I got to Travis AFB, I was rich. Further joy awaited me when I got the the itinerary of the plane. It was Hickum AB, Hawaii, Clark Air Base, PI and Tan Son Naht Air Base, South Vietnam.

You may be wondering why the inclusion of Clark Air Base was so significant. Well, remember Amilita, who lived in the PI. This way, I see Amy before going to Nam. For the first time in my life, I planned to do the wrong thing. My plan was to stay with my girl by missing the plane to Saigon from Clark AB. I had packed an AWOL (absence without leave) bag.

When the plane landed at Clark AB on December 23, 1966, I walked through the terminal, and hopped in a taxi, and went straight to Amy. After an hour of raw sex, I returned to the base terminal knowing full well that my plane had departed. My homeboy was on duty, so I told him my situation. He put me on the next plane. I convinced him that since it was the Christmas weekend, processing would be basically impossible. He agreed and rescheduled me for a flight on Wednesday. Well, Wednesday came and went. I saw my homeboy at the club. He told me if I did not get my ass on the next plane, he would turn me in himself. I was concerned but not worried. After all, what could the USAF do, put me in jail in the Philippines where I would be safe or send me to Nam to possibly get shot or blown to hell by a missile. The sick thing about my week in the PI was that when I got to Nam, they did not know I was coming. I could have stayed at Clark for the rest of my life.

My orders read 377th Civil Engineering Squadron (CES), Phu Cat AB. The personnel office told me my orders had a misprint because there was no such place as 377th CES or Phu Cat AB. The orders should have read 37th CES, Tan Son Naht AB. I said that if my orders had a misprint then maybe, I am not supposed to be here. Therefore, it is Phu Cat Air Base or Maxwell

Air Force Base, Alabama. For two weeks, I checked daily at the personnel office for a country deployment update. They finally found a teletype message confirming my orders. There was a proposed base (Phu Cat Air Base) with the personnel to be billeted at Qui Nhon Army Post. The chance of me returning home was shot to hell by a 4'×6"peice of paper. Isn't that SHIT?

The next day, I boarded a C-7A Caribou Plane for Qui Nhon Army Post and Phu Cat Air Base. During this time, only the RMK civilian workers were living at the Phu Cat site. Their job was to construct housing for the incoming military Prime Beef and Red Horse (Rapid Emergency Deployment Heavy Organization Squadron of Engineers) Civil Engineering Squadrons.

I got tired of that hour-long trip through hostile territory twice a day for two months. The crew could hardly wait for RMK to build enough barracks so we could move to the base for good. The buildings were finally complete and ready for occupancy. For a war zone, the barracks were quite modern but then it was the norm for USAF personnel to live great. We had indoor hot showers, washers, and dryers in every dorm and a bed with 6" thick mattresses. Our dining halls were second to none when it came to food. In fact, the food at Phi Cat was better than any stateside base I had visited. The base was situated in an area populated by the US Army and Marines. An air force base to those guys is like an in—country R&R (Rest and Recuperation) Center.

The army and the marines would come to Phu Cat to get a hot shower and a hot meal. But the air force personnel would still complain because they were so accustomed to luxury. I heard a US marine say to an airman, "Hell, son, the US Air Force invented *brunch*. So what the hell are you complaining about?" The USAF is the epitome of positive SHIT.

You know the average GI is like a dog in heat. During those two months in Qui Nhon, relationships developed. Therefore, the move to the base caused mixed emotions. You are right; I had gotten a girl and the thought of not seeing her daily was hard on a brother's two hearts. Her name was Huong. She would say, "My father was born in Laos and my mother was born in Cambodia, but I am a soul sister with the ass to prove it." Now you can understand my mixed emotions.

When we first moved to the base, equipment was rare. For instance, a lot of the work required a table saw. Our heavy tools had not arrived therefore, GI ingenuity came into play. I took a large hand saw and embedded it between two sheets of ¾ "plywood. I then used duct tape to hold the trigger in the on position. To turn the saw on and off, one had to plug and unplug the power cord. To make the correct measurements, a person had to measure out from the saw blade and then fasten a guide with a c-clamp. Because of the language barrier, the Vietnamese workers and I developed a language of our own. The word bombom was slang for sexual intercourse between the hookers and the GIs. Titi, a worker, and I decided to use the term bombom as a way to start the saw after all measurements and guides were in place. Well, one day, I was making some measurements by leaning over the blade. All of a sudden, the saw was plugged into the electrical socket. The sound of that saw scared the SHIT out of me. After I regained my composure, I jumped Titi's ass. With his broken English, he tried to explain that he heard me say "bombom." He was actually trying to kill me. I know he was out to kill me because two weeks later he was killed on the flight line throwing bombs under F-100 jet aircrafts. In all the good that we do as military personnel a VC (Viet Cong) will find a way to ensure SHIT.

During the rest of my tour, I was assigned the task of building 5,000 wooden wall lockers. The duty hours were from midnight until 0700 hours depending on the work load. Each night, a squadron would send a crew of twenty to the wood shop to construct the lockers. The dimensions of the lockers were 6' high, 8' long, 2 'thick, with 4 doors. You know that air force personnel must have a place to hang those starched and ironed jungle fatigues and the extra pair spit-shined jungle boots.

In Nam a lot of trading took place. Once I met helicopter pilot at a local hoe house in Qui Nhon. He and I talked about our jobs. When he found out that I was in charge of the lumberyard at midnight, his face lit up like a Christmas tree. He wanted to know what he could trade for two skids of ¾" plywood. I told him that my squadron (five-hundred men) needed C-rations and jungle fatigues. He agreed, and we had a deal. However, it would be his problem to get the wood off the base.

The next night at about 0200 hours, a large truck pulled into the lumberyard. This truck was loaded to the gill with cases and cases of rations and fatigues of all sizes. The sergeant said, "These are the supplies you ordered. I am to receive two skids of plywood." I told the sergeant we would help him unload the truck. He said, "Oh no! The truck is part of your supplies." At that moment, a huey helicopter landed in the woodyard to receive the plywood, and just like batman, he was up, up, and away. My first sergeant then traded the truck for a jeep, and the whole squadron received new fatigues and some C-rations for late-night snacks.

As I look back on my tour in Vietnam, the one thing that I thank God about most was the dumbest. Each morning after duty, I would rush to the barrack for a shower and change of clothes. I would then head to the main gate. Between 0800 and 0830 hours, a convoy of 175 mm self-propelled guns would pass by the base on their way to A Shaw Valley to do harassment firing. I would thumb a ride to a point halfway to Qui Nhon. Here was the dumbness on my part. There were some mornings when I stood on the road halfway between Qui Nhon and Phu Cat AB all by myself without even a knife for protection. Now, I look back and wonder, was it my upper head or my lower head controlling my mind? I liked Huong, but I loved Otha Mae's eldest son. This is a true case of the SHIT (stupidity has its time). As the old saying goes, "God takes care of old folks, babies, and fools." I had to have been the latter to wait unarmed, and all by myself in a war zone, for a piece of ass.

One morning, I decided not to go to Qui Nhon and hang out at the job. Well, that proved to be a great day because I got a chance to meet Lt. Gen. James Stewart of the Air National Guard. He is better known to most people by his screen name, Jimmy Stewart, a Hollywood movie star. General Stewart was on a tour to visit the troops in Nam.

When I finished my Vietnam tour, the shop gave me a going-away party with all the trimmings and all the booze and beer anyone could drink. This was the first and last time I drank in Nam. I promised my fellow airmen that I would get drunk with them before going home. I got sloppy drunk on canadian club and ginger ale. The reason I never drank while in Vietnam was because I do not drink alcohol, period. The other reason I never drink in Nam was because if Charlie (Viet Cong) came over the hill, I would know where to run.

The best going-away gift I received from Vietnam was from a young lady in Qui Nhon. She took an American silver dollar and melted it into a ring. She then had the ring inscribed with Huong/Wimes and presented it to me as a farewell gift. She showed she really cared for me.

I went to Vietnam as A2C James Wimes, and now, it was time for me to leave Nam as Sergeant James Wimes. With three days left in Nam, I decided to spend two with my war friends. After all, there were C-7 caribou aircraft going back and forth to Cam Ranh Bay Air Base every three hours. The first day, I visited both Prime Beef and Red Horse sections of Phu Cat, the base I had helped build. It was like leaving one of your own. For some unknown reason, I just went to the terminal and quietly left without any fanfare. Two hours later, I was at Cam Ranh Bay Air Base waiting for my flight to the Philippines. I checked into the billeting office for a hooch (hard back tent) and a bed for the two days I had left in Vietnam. That night, while lying in my bed, watching the rats the size of cats play in the rafters and praying they didn't fall, the radio got my attention. Hanoi Hannah started her brainwashing talk show. She started by saying that the GIs at Phu Cat will not eat or watch movies tonight. Their new outdoor theater and dining hall was just blown to hell. The thought that I almost stayed two more days there scared the true shit out of me.

My plane, with a stopover at the Philippines, was not scheduled to leave for two days. I got up, put on my uniform, packed my bags, and headed for the air terminal. Hanoi Hannah's broadcast had convinced me it was time to leave Nam and as soon as possible. The flight clerk said there was a C-141 cargo plane bound for McChord AFB, Washington, leaving in three hours. At that moment, my only thought was Inez Gamble, the woman, and the family that had kept me going with letters and boxes of food from down south. My love came down and I was homebound. When that C-141 touched down on American land and opened the door to good old USA, I got off and kissed the pavement. The main thing is another American GI had outlived SHIT.

I still had another 3000 miles to get to Macon, Georgia, and Inez. But at that moment, Seattle was all the home I needed. The bus ride from McChord AFB to SEA-TAC Airport left me with one memory. There was a giant sign that read, "If you are the last one to leave, turn out the light." Well, I left the light on because there were many fellow servicemen in Nam that would be coming home through McChord AFB, Washington, back home to the USA.

The plane ride home had a layover in Chicago, where Joyce Akridge now lived and worked. I decided to give her a call for old times' sake. She talked me into staying for three days. I checked into the fabulous Drake Hotel for two days. Joyce and I went out for dinner and conversation. On the third day, I flew to LA (Lovely Atlanta) for a short bus trip to Macon. My family was very proud of me coming home as a sergeant. Inez, on the other hand, was angry because I stopped in Chitown. After much begging, and a lot of "I'm sorry's", we smoothed things over and were back in sync.

However, my happiness was cut short. One day, I went to visit Inez, and as soon as I entered the house, I knew something was wrong. This was the fourth day of my visit to Inez. She said, "James, you need to go home. Something has happened." I knew then it was my great-grandmother. Hattie Hill and I were a pair ever since I could remember. She had counseled me the day before on the virtues of marriage to a sweet girl like Inez. Ma Hattie told me she was married to four men and never divorced any one. She said she loved them all to death. In the twenty minutes that it took to drive across town, my great-grandmother and best friend had gone to heaven. Ma Hattie had been sick for a long time. The family said she was just waiting for her favorite son to come home. Before I arrived from Nam, Ma Hattie could not recognize her own daughters. The minute I walked into the house, her face lit up with a smile. I loved that old lady, and I know she is in the bosom of God. However, the loss of that sweet old woman goes to show that SHIT.

While in Vietnam, I saved my money through saving bonds and the military saving program where the government matches your savings 50/50. I saved enough money to buy a 1967 Mercury Cougar for cash. The car was to be Inez's wedding present. All the money was at the Maxwell AFB Credit

Union. I went to Montgomery to buy the car. I stayed at the same Albert Picks Hotel where I contacted STD a year earlier. The cougar I bought was canary yellow with black interior. The call to Inez proved to be a bad idea. She heard female voices in the background of my hotel room. The marriage was off. Inez did not want to hear anything I had to say. Our relationship was over. I lost my great-grandmother and future wife in less than two weeks. If that isn't it, I don't know what this SHIT is!

CHAPTER 7

The Sunshine State of Florida

A few days later, I drove to my new assignment at MacDill AFB, Florida. When I processed into the base as a sergeant, "there was no room at the inn." At first the thought of living off base upset me. Then the clerk told me that I would be living in a contract hotel off base. They sent me to the Bay shore Royal Hotel on the beautiful bayshore blvd. in downtown Tampa, Florida. Tampa is located on the Gulf of Mexico. The hotel overlooked the famous Tampa Bay.

Folklore has it that pirates sailed into Tampa Bay and raped most of the women and robbed most of the men. Since that time, each year the people of Tampa celebrate Gasparilla Pirate Fest. During the week, they have parades, circus, and parties throughout the city in honor of Jose Gaspar and his pirates.

It did not take me long to be introduced to the night life in Tampa. My roommate had me follow him to West Tampa. He led me down Howard Avenue to Main Street and into the Ebony Lounge. This night club was where an airman could get a "hookup." My roommate (Howard) and I got separated because he met his hookup and left the club. I knew we had come straight down Howard Avenue, but when I tried to return to the hotel, I discovered it was a one-way street. Now, I got lost because Tampa is a one-way street Mecca. I drove up and down Main Street trying to find my way back to the hotel.

I noticed that a young lady started blowing the horn of her car. I pulled over to the right thinking something was wrong with my new cougar. Ms. Rorry Cannon pulled in beside me. She said, "I just wanted to see the man driving the yellow cougar." She asked if I wanted a cup of coffee. She lived on Main Street with her mother and grandmother. That night we had several cups of coffee and we talked until 04:00hrs. It was getting very late, and I still did not know my way home. I asked Rorry if she knew a quick way to get to the Bayshore Royal Hotel. She smiled and said, "Turn right at the next street, which is Green Street, and go straight to Bayshore Blvd and turn right to the hotel."

Rorry and I became a couple. She was thick in the hips and very sweet in the lips. My new girlfriend also possessed the largest pair of mammary glands I had ever seen. She and I would take turns sharing one another's bed. Of course, when I slept over at her house, I was very uncomfortable with her mother and grandmother in their rooms across the hall.

I had died and gone to heaven in Tampa, Fla. I was a GI driving a brand new car. I was living in a luxury hotel with daily maid service. I was dating a lady with beautiful breasts who loved to cook. On top of all that, Tampa, Florida, had warm weather almost every day. Oh, I didn't die. The Sunshine State of Florida was a piece of heaven. By the way, Lt. Gen. Benjamin O. Davis, Jr. was the vice commander of Strike Command.

One afternoon, the NCOIC called me in from the shooting range. He said that I had been selected for guard duty on a rescue boat. I called Rorry and told her she could keep my baby (car) for the rest of the night because I had guard duty. She drove me to the dockyard, and we kissed good-bye. I took my post. With a ship-to-shore phone, guard duty, and the next day off was not a bad deal. After settling in for the night, all was well until 2100 hours when there was a shout from shore, "may I board?" The biggest black colonel I had ever seen stepped on board. He identified himself as Colonel Daniel "Chappy" James. I came to attention and saluted. He began asking me questions such as, "Where is your weapon?" "Did you have lunch?" "How long are you going to be on duty?" He got angrier with every answer I gave, but not at me. He said, "I will send someone to relieve you at midnight."

At about 2330 hours, a Lt Colonel (O5) dressed in Class A formal air force uniform came aboard the boat. He asked the same questions Col. James had asked. He too got angry. The thought of an O5 sent to relieve an E4 for guard duty worried the stink out of me. I told the light colonel that I would be glad to stay and finish the night. He said, "No, I am going to relieve you and be here in these dress blues. This way, when I go in tomorrow morning, I will be really pissed off with that fat ass master sergeant who is responsible for me, the vice base commander, pulling guard duty."

I called Rorry to pick me up as soon as possible. While waiting for her, the Lt. Colonel explained that MacDill AFB had lost three F-4 phantom fighters, one in Tampa Bay and two in the Gulf of Mexico. He also pointed out that Col. James was the chief investigator on those accidents. For those that don't know, Col. James went on to become the first black Four Star General in the US military and the Commander of NORAD. You can also bet your money that the fat ass master sergeant knows the true meaning of SHIT.

As time passed, I got to know many more people in Tampa. What with my car and living in a luxury hotel, I was exposed to several women. The fairest of them all was a Cuban-born lady named, Angelica Gonzalez. She spent more time in my room than she did in her own home. It was okay because she loved to cook, and I loved to eat. This lovely lady was married with children, so I had the best of both worlds, Angelica in the day and Rorry at night.

Everything was going great until one Friday afternoon, I was told over the mobile radio to report to the orderly room as soon as possible. The first shirt said I had special orders for deployment. I told the first sergeant I am prepared to go to jail before going back to Vietnam. He said he did not know where we were going but the deployment was not Nam base on the equipment, the supply section was to issue my partner and me. We felt special when told supply and finance were being held open just for two individuals, Peter Wetakowicks and me. We were issued open pay orders, a complete brand new set of carpentry tools, and finally extreme cold weather gear, including bunny boots. At that moment, I knew we were not going to Vietnam or anywhere in SE Asia. My orders read to report to Eglin AFB, Florida for intensive Red Horse Training.

What to do with my car when I go to parts unknown was now my major concern. My play brother, Richard Appling, was right up the street at Albany State College, Georgia. The cougar was loaded, but first, I had to visit Rorry. She had to know about my emergency deployment. She cried and did not understand how I could not know where I was going. She took my head and laid it between her large breasts for some good going-away love. She started crying a second time, but there was nothing we could do. That Thursday night, I drove to Georgia to talk to Richard. I got there early in the morning. He had classes on Friday, the day I was to report for training. He could drive me to Eglin AFB, after classes late Friday evening.

That morning I went to the student center to meet Richard. We were to have lunch. While waiting for him, I spotted an amazonian-looking woman. I could not take my eyes off her. She was tall with a wild afro hairstyle. Richard finally arrived. My first question was, "Who is that stallion over there in the food line?" We call her Bert, but her full name is Alberta Bell. You will be wasting your time because we have been begging her for three years. I told Richard, "You introduce me, and I will do the rest." The one thing I know about women is that they all love to eat. I told Alberta that I was there to visit my brother, Richard Appling. He had classes for the rest of the afternoon and I was starving. Would she be interested in having a good lunch with me? Alberta responded with a resounding, "Yes, because this college food sucks." She directed me to the Cabin in the Pines. A small juke joint that served down home fried chicken gizzards and wings. We ate like pigs. Alberta said she was stuffed and ready to sleep.

Richard had given me the keys to his apartment in case I got bored on campus. Bert and I went to the apartment after a great meal. I told her that I was leaving the next day for an overseas assignment. Alberta pulled back the bed covers and got in with her clothes still intact. I stripped down to my t shirt and drawers before getting in bed beside her.

As one thing led to another, she realized I wanted to make love to her. As I fumbled undressing her, she became frustrated and said to me, "Do you want me to help you?" That afternoon was the greatest going-away present I ever received. Alberta and I spent the rest of the afternoon lying in one another's arms in total bliss.

At 1630 hours, the door opened and Dorothy Lampkin (Dot) stuck her head in the door and then disappeared. Alberta and I quickly got dressed. She made up the bed, and we returned to the student's center. When we arrived, Dot was raising hell with Richard about being in bed with a woman. Poor Richard could not defend himself for laughing. The more he laughed, the madder Dot got. He knew what Dot had seen was Alberta and me. He finally convinced Dot to look towards the entrance of the student center where Bert and I were standing. All Dot could say was, "Why didn't you tell me James was in town? I feel like a pure fool."

The four of us went back to Richard's apartment where I explained that I needed him to keep my car while I was overseas. I would pay the note on the car but he would have to pay the insurance. However, he needed to drive me to Eglin AFB, Florida, as soon as possible because I was already two days late. Richard quickly agreed. After all, he was being given the opportunity to sport a new 1967 canary yellow cougar around Albany State College. Without being in the military Richard benefited from SHIT.

CHAPTER 8

Red Horse in Korea

The next morning, I reported to the Red Horse Training Center. The First Sergeant greeted me with a strong, "Where in the hell have you been? You were supposed to be here yesterday." As I started to explain, there was a familiar voice that I had not heard in several years say, "Sgt. Wimes, what are you doing here?" The voice came from Col. James W. Baxter. He told the First Sergeant that he would deal with me. I was glad to see that tall white man because my ass was grass and the First Sergeant had the lawn mower. The Colonel and I reminisced about the rebuilding of the Mactan Air Base in the southern Philippine Islands. Just to give you a piece of history, Mactan Island is the burial site of Ferdinand Magellan. There is a memorial about fifty yards off the coast of Mactan Island. Legend has it that the famous explorer was killed by a tribal chief for disrespecting the princess daughter of the chief.

I asked the Colonel, "Where are we going?" He would only tell me that the mission was top secret, but it was not Vietnam. The colonel also said we had two months to train for this assignment. The training would commence at 0500 hours Monday morning. That Sunday, we shacked up at our living quarters and got some rest.

Five in the morning comes very quickly. Our first briefing was at 0600 hours, immediately after breakfast. At 0700 hours we were divided into ten fifty-men training units. We marched or jogged from one class to the other. The first two weeks was all physical training (PT)—Bomb Damage Repair (BDR) and self-defense classes. We worked from 0500hrs to 1800 hours with a one-hour break for lunch and thirty minutes for breakfast. At night, we were allowed to leave Eglin Field Three.

One night, a group of horses (GIs) decided to go into Niceville, Florida, to party at this night club. Being military personnel, we forgot that in 1968 some places in the State of Florida still had problems with the integration of races. When we arrived at the club as part of a diverse group, we were told blacks were not allowed. We boarded the 6 × 6 truck to return to Field Three. That night, I made a lifelong friend. His name was George Season, a 6'4", 280 pounds, white man from Arkansas. He was embarrassed by the incident. The closer we got to the training camp the madder this big white man got. SSgt. George Season broke into the shed and took three or four smoke bombs. Several of us returned to the club to support George. He threw two of the grenades into the club. As each man exited the club, George stood there like John Henry driving steel on a railroad. He drove a left and right fist for about five minutes into every racist that came out of the door.

The news beat us back to the base. Col. Baxter held a squadron meeting the next morning at 0600 hours. He started by saying, "I am going to find out who stole the grenades and put them in jail." He then asked whether we won the fight. I believe the colonel knew exactly who the huge white man was based on the description.

A few weeks later, George asked me if I liked country and western music. I said, "Hell, no!" At the time, he was listening to a song. "Kiss an Angel Good morning." George shouted out, "Listen to that soul brother sing." I thought he had lost his mind. There was no way a black man could sing that country. George and I argued half the night. Three days later, George rushed into the barrack and inquired if I had any money to lend him. Naturally, I wanted to know how much. Three dollars was his reply. We then walked across the street to the BX (Base Exchange). He led me to the magazine rack. On the cover of Country Music magazine was a picture of the number one singer in country and western music. It was a black man, Mr. Charlie Pride and his number one hit was, "Kiss an Angel Good Morning." All I could say to George was, SHIT.

We finally finished the ten weeks of training. Sgt. James E. Wimes had reached the pinnacle of Civil Engineering. I was now RED HORSE qualified. There were several red horse units such as 819th, 820th, 555th, and now 557th. It was still top secret as to where this new unit would be deployed. However, in late March 1968, a large stretch DC-8 arrived at Eglin AFB, Florida, to take around three-hundred-and-fifty Red Horse qualified men to parts unknown. Our first stop was Elmendolf AFB, Alaska, to refuel. The team then flew to Norita Airport, Tokyo, Japan. It was over Tokyo that we experienced our first problem. It was also the first time we came to know the destination of the team. We were headed for Osan AB, Korea.

North Korea had taken the USS Pueblo and had refused to release the crew. We (557th Red Horse) were being deployed to South Korea, more specifically, Kung Ju Air Base. Our job was to reopen the base for other military groups which were to be sent to the Pacific. It was the USS Pueblo incident that caused the Japanese government to refuse landing rights to our DC-8 aircraft in Japan. The Japanese Government did not want to get involved in any conflict with North Korea.

Finally, the plane was allowed to land for emergency refueling only and only the aircraft crew was allowed to deplane. That day, airline safety was compromised. The plane was refusal with more than 300 pax on board. That was a new paradigm in SHIT.

Once we cleared Japanese air space, Col. Baxter briefed the team. He said, "We were one of the first military deployments to South Korea to take back our ship and crew." He told us that Commander Bucher and the crew were waiting for us to come and get them out of North Korea. The flight from Japan to Osan AB, South Korea, takes about ninety minutes. Once we arrived, the first thing we were told was that, "if you want somewhere to sleep, you have to build it." We went into action as we had been trained.

In less than five hours, 557th RED HORSE was bedded down for the night. We had built thirty ten-men hard-backed tents, enough for three hundred enlisted men. The officers lived in the BOQ (Bachelor Officers Quarters). After flying almost thirty hours and building thirty hooches, one would think sleep would be the only option. We walked two blocks, took a shower, changed our fatigues, and headed for the main gate in 10 degrees weather. We passed several night clubs, but the black troops were told that the brothers hung out at a club called Papa Joe's Lounge. Needless to say, Papa Joes was the last joint on the strip. I knew I was in the right place when I heard James Brown's Band playing "Mono Rail."

The funny thing about our trip was that we had not been told where we were going until we left Japan. However, as soon as we entered the club there was a gigantic sign reading "Welcome 557th RED HORSE" hung above the bar. Some of the ladies of the evening even had little red horse stamps on their cheeks, top and bottom. Osan Air Base was the best assignment in South Korea basically because of its close proximity to Seoul. There is a shopping Mecca known as E Tai Won in Seoul. In E Tai Won, a person could buy right from a pencil to a large carat diamond ring at reasonable prices. As you know, I love clothes. While in Korea, I bought Nike sneakers, jogging suits, luggage, and mink blankets for the entire family.

While we were halfway around the world preparing for a possible war with North Korea, a man was waiting to assassinate a great leader. He was not a leader of nations but a King and a leader of people. He was Dr. Martin Luther King, Jr. He had gone to Memphis, Tennessee, to assist the sanitation workers. On the morning of April 4, 1968, the King stood on the balcony of the Lorraine Motel when he was assassinated by a white man who killed a dream.

All hell broke loose throughout the world, even in Korea. There were racial fights at almost every military installation between people of color and whites. Col. Baxter convened a quick Red Horse squadron meeting. He reminded us of that incident in Niceville, Florida, where a lone white man fought for the rights of the black members of 557th Red Horse. He said he would not tolerate any member of our team fighting among themselves. "The assassination of Rev. Dr. King is living proof that civilians can experience SHIT."

My tour to Osan Air Base was short-lived because Col. Baxter knew I was the best floor tile installer on the team. He directed me to take the next mule train to Kwang Ju Air Base. My task was to retile the Base Headquarter Building. Kwang Ju was a more conservative part of Korea. It lacked the warmth of hot women, but made up with a warmer climate. It took me about three weeks to complete the work in the headquarter building.

Col. Baker visited Kwang Ju one day to check on the troops. He told us about the softball team at Osan. This was my chance to get back to hot women and hot food. I told him that his softball championship was at Kwang Ju. The best pitcher is SSgt. George Season and best first baseman is Sgt. James Wimes. The colonel gave us two hours to pack for the return trip to Osan Air Base. Yes, Red Horse defeated the Supply Squadron in the Base Softball Championship.

The summer of 1968 gave way to fall, and I kept asking when we would go home to the USA. I was told this deployment was for six months only. I was ready to get back to the States for collard greens, ham hocks and cornbread, not to mention Rorry and her rack. After several weeks of soon, soon, and very soon, I wrote a letter to Senator Rickard B. Russell of Georgia. I just wanted to know, "how the US Air Force could come up with five-hundred men in forty-eight hours for deployment and could not come up with five-hundred replacements for the same men in six months."

In late September 1968, I was at a female friend's house in Osan City when my partner Josea Washington knocked on the door. He said that the colonel was looking for me because I had orders to return home. I got dressed, and went to the base to check in, and was told that my name had been removed from the list. That was fine with me because I was not ready to leave Korea that day. I went back down town. A few minutes later, Sgt. Washington knocked and when I answered the second time Washingston was out of breath. Col. Baxter had given him direct orders, "to find Sgt. Wimes and put his ass on the next plane to the States." Senator Russell had inquired about the length of his tour in Korea. Col. Baker was somewhat upset with me for having written to the senator before briefing him.

The good thing about the extended stay in Korea was that I got credit for a short overseas tour. There is an air force regulation that says any temporary duty that lasts for more than a hundred-eighty days is considered a short overseas tour. The only problem with going home was the short notice of my departure. It would have been easier on the emotions if adequate time to say good-bye had been available. The average Red Horse member will almost never have the time to bid his family and friends a hearty farewell because of the "R" in Red Horse. That "R" means Rapid and in most cases rapid means "right now." Red Horse men have to endure SHIT.

Chapter 9

Georgia on My Mind

With Georgia on my mind, I departed from Korea. I headed straight to Macon, Georgia, to pick up my car. My play sister, Nettie, had been building me up with another beautiful young lady named Ruby McIvery. Ruby came to Macon to teach high school. She was a graduate from Albany State College. I arrived home in time for her homecoming festivities. Dot Lampkin and Richard Appling had gotten married while I was in Korea. Dot had written me a letter telling me that Alberta Bell was expecting to deliver the baby that I had fathered. I wrote Alberta several times but she never responded.

Ruby and I went to Albany for the homecoming parade and football game. While at the parade, I ran into Alberta. She was still as beautiful as she was the first time I laid eyes upon her. However, she was in her eighth month of pregnancy. She and I talked during the parade but we needed more in depth conversation concerning the baby. I gave Alberta the phone number to my hotel room so we could finish our conversation. Ruby and I decided to get separate rooms in case she wanted to entertain her Delta sisters.

The problem occurred when the hotel operator transferred Alberta's call to Ruby's room. Then it was on. Ruby asked, "Why are you calling my man and especially in my hotel room." Alberta responded with, "I called because I am about to deliver his baby." I wondered how to explain to Ruby that Alberta and I had a one-afternoon-stand nine months back just before I left for Korea. Ruby was so upset she returned to Macon on a Greyhound Bus. She even left her new Chevy Camaro with me in Albany. I finally got to talk to Alberta. She told me the baby she was carrying was mine. She also said that I need not worry because she was going to marry a sailor. The same sailor she was dating before she met me. She said, "I told my fiancée that the baby was not his." The sailor wanted to marry her anyway. Alberta's future husband is the personification of SHIT.

Ruby refused to talk to me when I returned to Macon. She only wanted me to return the keys to her 1968 sky-blue camaro. Needless to say, homecoming at ASC was a bust. I tried once again to talk to Ruby. She informed me that it was over between us. I drove my car to I-75 and headed south to Tampa, Florida. Ruby was not the first teacher to dump me. Remember Inez Gamble, the woman I wanted to marry in 1966. Well just to give you an update. Inez moved to East Orange, New Jersey, and married a member of the Appling family.

As I settled back into my job of tiling floors and patching roofs, life returned to normal. During the week, I dated Rorry and Floritina. However, Rorry and I began to put some distance between us. One Sunday morning, Rorry's grandmother asked me to take her to the grocery store. While in the store, Rorry and her new man walked in. I told her to go get in my car. She went outside and I followed. She and I argued until her new friend came to defend her. He had a pistol in his hand. He first tried to pistol-whip me. Thanks to my RED HORSE self-defense training and physical conditioning, I was able to take his pistol and beat his ass. Later that afternoon, I gave the pistol to Rorry's grandmother. From that day, Rorry had no significance in my life. Georgia stayed on my mind now more than ever because my piece of heaven was turning into hell. I went home to Georgia every weekend to visit my family and friends.

One day, a young airman walked into the carpentry shop and said he was looking for Sgt Wimes. I introduced myself and he introduced himself as A2C Peter Blaylock. He wanted to know if he could hitch a ride with me to Georgia.

He said he could take a bus to Atlanta from there to visit his family. He said he would share the expenses and the driving. I was ecstatic. Peter became my road dog. We went home every weekend. One weekend, Peter decided to stay in Macon and hang out with my family. He had some feelings for my sister. Both Patricia and Peter stuttered very badly. It most hilarious to hear the two of them talk. It would take five minutes for them to greet each other. It was the funniest SHIT.

Once, Blaylock and I decided to stop at Albany State College to visit some of my friends. I ran into Renilda Wilson, a girl I knew from my high school. Even then she wanted to make me her boyfriend. Renilda was a pretty girl with a weight problem. Above all, she was a home girl. She took us around ASC and introduced Peter and me to several of her associates. There was one young lady I met from St. Petersburg, Florida. Her name was Aurrelia Harris.

Aurrelia and I became friends and remain so even today. She was a transfer student from Xavier University in New Orleans, which she left because there her brother kept her in line. At ASC she was free to attend or not to attend classes. She had a sister, Lorraine, who lived in Atlanta, and she would often ride to Tampa with Blaylock and me to visit her mother for the week. Aurrelia graduated from ASC, University of Florida, and earned a doctorate from Michigan State in Agriculture Economy. She went on to teach at several colleges before landing a government job in New Mexico.

I once visited Aurrelia while she was a student at University of Florida. I witnessed a sadistic scene there that I remember to this day. The night before, a young man went swimming in the hotel pool. He never returned to his room. His wife and son waited in vain; the gentleman had drowned. It was sad for me to watch that three-year-old boy calling out to his daddy who was lying still in the water. All I could do was cry for the wife and the son of the dead military man. You may wonder how I knew he was in the military. When the police were investigating the incident they inspected his car which had a military NCO vehicle pass on the windshield. This military family had experienced the ultimate in SHIT.

One day, Blaylock asked if we were going to Georgia that weekend. My response was a flat "no" because I didn't have any money. Pete Blaylock stuttered for about ten minutes explaining to me that we could sell our blood to the blood bank to get gas money. On Thursday, he and I went to the county blood bank. We discovered that Blaylock had type O+ and I was type B+. Blaylock got angry when I was paid fifty dollars and he was paid only twenty dollars. Apparently, B+ was semi-rare and therefore, it was worth more. Pete stuttered angrily all the way back to the base for being cheated by the blood bank. However, between paydays we sold blood to finance our trips to Georgia.

One week in Tampa, and two weeks later, we went across the bridge to St. Petersburg.

Pete and I drove to Macon one weekend and went directly to visit Mrs. Daisy Appling better known as Parent. Parent always had something to eat for wandering travelers. Fannie, the youngest of Parent's three children, was home from college for a medical appointment. She asked if I would drive her back to Fort Valley State College. The college was about thirty miles south of Macon in the direction we had passed an hour earlier. Fannie begged and pleaded with me to drive her to school. She finally produced the incentive needed for the ride. She said that the school had about four-hundred freshmen girls and she was in charge of their dorm. She said she would introduce Blaylock and me to them if we drove her to school. We agreed to make the short trip.

When we arrived on campus in front of the library, she jumped from the car laughing and ran into the building. She had made a fool out of us. So we decided to drive around the campus to check out the eye candy (girls). This was early fall, and the candy was out in full blossom. Blaylock spotted a female friend he knew from Atlanta. Her name was Louise Simmons. She took us to the senior dorm. As Pete renewed old friendships, I sat in the commons area and continued to enjoy the beautiful black ladies.

After a few minutes, I spied the real girl of my dreams. I asked Louise, "Who is that angel?" She whispered, "Miss Lockhart." I called out to the young lady, "Miss Lockhart, may I speak with you?" This lady was so pretty. The most unique thing about this young lady was the color of her eyes and her skin tone. She had a light-brown complexion with bright, green eyes. I was in love.

When she came over to me, her first question was, "How do you know my name?" I told her a little bird told me her last name and no she didn't know me. However, I said that I didn't know her either, but would like to get to know her. She said her name was Velma Lockhart. Then I introduced myself as Sgt. James Ellis Wimes. We talked for more than an hour. Velma then said she had to go to her sorority meeting. She was the basileus (president) of Zeta Phi Beta of Fort Valley State College, and she had to be there.

Velma had not been gone ten minutes when another cute young lady strolled through the commons. I looked to Louise and made the same inquiry about this new piece of eye candy. Louise said her name was Miss Clements. I used the exact same line on her that I had used on Velma. Miss Cements and I talked for a few moments and then she departed. It was then that Miss Simmons decided to tell me that Miss Lockhart and Miss Clements were roommates.

Miss Lockhart reappeared as Miss Clements disappeared around the corner. "That was a quick meeting," I said to Velma. She smiled and said that the sorors had other things to do and beside this gave her more time to talk with me. At that moment, I knew I had hit on something great. I went back to the time when I met Alberta Bell. I was on a college campus with a pretty woman so ask her out to dinner. She and I had our first dinner date at "What-A-Burger Drive-In."

Velma and I made a cute couple. We talked on the phone Monday through Thursday, despite knowing that I was going to make that more-than-three-hundred-mile drive on Friday. My phone bill and my gas bill kept me broke. The best idea I came up with was to contract with a friend to rent a room in his apartment. I only wanted to use the space on weekends. It was a lot cheaper to share the expense for the apartment than pay for a hotel two nights a week. My mother had promised to give me a bedroom suite when I got married. Since it appeared that I was never getting married, she gave me the bedroom set for the apartment. We would spend the every weekend together for the rest of Velma's school year.

To go back to the little Zeta from Garden Valley, Georgia, I picked Velma up every Friday around 2200 hours. We went to the apartment and talked until 0100hours. You may be wonder why we didn't just go to the apartment and hang out for the rest of the weekend. During those days, even senior girls living in the dorms had to have a letter on file from parents to spend the night out. The letter had to be on file for a week before the weekend outing. That rule changed for senior girls in January, 1969. That is when Velma and I started spending every weekend at the apartment or traveling to different colleges throughout Georgia. Our relationship grew stronger and stronger.

However, Velma was not giving up any part of her drawers. In fact, she and I slept in the same bed from fall until spring, but sex was out of the question. The spring of 1969 was so wonderful and particularly in Fort Valley, Georgia, the peach capital of the world. Spring also meant the eye candy was back in full blossom. During my eye candy stroll, I met a fine young freshman from Thomasville, Georgia. I started seeing her every chance I got. Little did I know that one of Velma's sorors was the student dean at the freshman dormitory. Needless to say, Velma was upset that I was spending a lot of time in the freshmen area.

The following weekend, I picked Velma up and went to dinner. She and I laughed and talked about past events at Fort Valley State College. We reminisced about the time Louise Simmons caught her boyfriend with another girl in his car. He dropped the girl at the dorm, drove to his house off campus, got undressed, and was in bed pretending to be sick, all in less than ten minutes. From that day on, we called him Superman. After dinner, we went to the apartment for bed.

I took off my clothes and got into bed. Making love to Velma Lockhart was the farthest from my mind. After all, I had been conditioned for six months that I could touch, rub, and play with the candy as long as it stayed in the wrapper (her drawers). That particular night, Velma had other plans. I suspect she felt that she would be the joke of the campus if she allowed a freshman take her man. She started undressing with the lights still bright. She saw the look on my face and said, "Don't you want me to get undressed?" For a brief moment, I felt like Gerry Coleman of Different Strokes, "What you talking about Velma?" Well the wrappers were off and the candy was sweet and well worth the wait. When the weekend was over that Sunday, I drove Velma to her dormitory about 1600 hours. As I headed south on Interstate 75, all I could think of was I am a SHIT.

The more time I spent with Velma, the more time I wanted to be with her. There were times when I had to work for half a day on Saturday, but at noon, I would head north to FVSC to see Velma. I knew full well that in less than twenty-four hours, I would have to make the reverse trip back to Tampa, Florida. Velma could have made me do anything when she smiled at me with those green eyes. Her eyes also put the females in Florida in the history books. All my thoughts were on the lady with green eyes, the lady from Tote Over Creek, near Reynolds, Georgia. The lady was Miss Velma Jean Lockhart.

While at work one afternoon, I was summoned to the orderly room. Once there, the chief clerk informed me that I had orders for overseas. This did not matter to me because Velma and I had discussed about my taking a discharge at the end of my current enlistment. I asked the clerk as to where I was posted. He said, "APO 96274." I knew immediately that APO 96274 was Clark Air Base, Philippines. For me to take the assignment, I would have to reenlist for another four years. I accepted the assignment and couldn't wait to get home to call and tell Velma. She had mixed emotions to the news. She was happy that I was going to the Philippines because she knew from our many conversations that I truly enjoyed my previous assignment there. She was sad because she knew I would be leaving her. I promised her we would discuss further over the weekend when we were together.

TSgt. Palmer, who was once my training instructor in basic gave me the afternoon off that Friday so I could get home earlier. At about 1800 hours, I arrived at FVSC. Velma was packed and ready to go to Macon. As usual, we went to dinner for some romantic conversation. However, this night was super special because it was the night that I would end Velma's anxieties. She was still troubled about my assignment to the PI. She suggested that I get out of the USAF and attend college. She would be graduating in two months. She would get a job and support us while I get a college degree. It sounded good but my ego would not let a lady take care of me.

I asked Velma, "How would you feel about this assignment if you could go with me?" Those beautiful eyes lit up like a Christmas tree. My marriage proposal was somewhat unusual, but Velma understood that I was asking her to marry me. Her answer was as unusual as my proposal. She never said "yes." However, that night she started making wedding plans. That night, we set the wedding date for August 16, 1969. From that night until the wedding, Velma glowed with happiness.

Velma could not wait to give the news to her best friend, Carolyn Burris. The following weekend, we went to Macon to visit family and friends. Carolyn lived across the street from Velma's sister, Savannah. When we arrived at Carolyn's house, she told us that she had seen Velma in Macon on several occasions riding in a yellow car. Carolyn had told even Savannah that she thought she had seen Velma in Macon. Savannah vehemently denied Carolyn's statement because she had been in school at FVSC. Carolyn on the other hand knew she was not crazy when she saw Velma and me drive up in a 1967 yellow cougar.

Getting back to the news, Velma and Carolyn could not wait to tell one another. Carolyn started talking first. She said, "Velma, Burris (her husband) got an assignment to the Philippines Islands and I am going with him." Velma's green eyes opened wide with joy. She looked at Carolyn and said I had also got an assignment overseas and that she will also be going to PI.

"Where are you all going?" asked Carolyn. We are going to Clark Air Base, Philippine Islands, after we get married on August 16 (1969),. The two of them hugged and rejoiced with one another like to kids in a candy store.

Velma graduated in June, 1969, with a degree in English, and a minor in Music. We were planning our wedding but there was a problem said my future wife. The problem was with Savannah Lockhart, Senior. Mrs. Lockhart was one of the richest women in Garden Valley, Georgia. Mrs. Lockhart was concerned over the marriage of her youngest daughter and the baby of her sixteen children. According to Velma, her mother stated, "the fifteen brothers and sisters wanted to know when their baby sister was getting married." Mrs. Lockhart told the siblings she did not know because James had not yet asked for Vel's hand in marriage. I continued to visit Velma throughout the summer at her family estate. The house was about twenty miles south of Reynolds, Georgia. The house was located approximately two miles from the main road. Her father owned all the land which was full of cotton, peanuts, sweet potatoes, and watermelon right from the road to beyond the house. In late June, 1969, I decided to honor her mother's wishes. One afternoon, I sat at the kitchen table with Velma and her mother. I thought it was now or never. I was going to ask for permission to marry the baby of this well-respected family.

I started off by telling my future mother-in-law about my inexperience in proposing. I said, "As you know, I have never done this before, so do I have your permission to marry Velma."

S.H.I.T—Servicemen Have It Tough

Mrs. Lockhart said, "Yes, but you have to also ask her father." She sent Velma to the field to get her father, Mr. James Lockhart or Professor Lockhart as was known. He came in the house and requested for some peaches with sugar sprinkled over them. As Mrs. Lockhart prepared the peaches, she explained she and I had been talking about the wedding. Mr. Lockhart quickly responded with, "Were you and James talking, or was it just you talking." Mr. Lockhart looked me directly in the eyes and made this profound statement, "James, if Velma loves you, she is going to marry you with or without our permission. So this is a useless conversation. Savannah, may I have some more peaches." I went to visit the Lockhart estate each weekend until August 16, 1969 when we all met at St. Peter Claver Catholic Church for the wedding. The honeymoon was to be in a quaint little motel, south of Macon, Georgia.

The more I visited the Lockharts, the more I liked the patriarch. I nicknamed Mr. Lockhart, "Daddy Cool." That man would not let anything bother him. For instance, one weekend, I was sitting on the front porch when Mr. Elijah Simmons came to the house with a message from the youngest son who lives in Atlanta. Mr. Simmons was a white neighbor who lived on the main road, which was over two miles away. Before I continue with this story, let me explain why the Lockharts did not have a house phone. The telephone company felt the house was too far from the road to run a single phone line for a black family. Anyway, Mr. Simmons said that Paul had called and asked him to tell his father to call back because it was an emergency.

Mr. Lockhart was in the field, hand dusting his one bale cotton crop when Velma and I went to deliver the message. Daddy Cool was his usual self. He said, "Well, if Paul is sick, he should have called a doctor, if Paul is in jail, he is safe, and if he is dead, there is absolutely nothing I can do for him now. When I finish dusting my cotton, I will go call him." This man, my father-in-law, was a man I would love to have had as a military commander because he never broke under pressure not to mention SHIT.

Chapter 10

The Philippines; Start of a Family

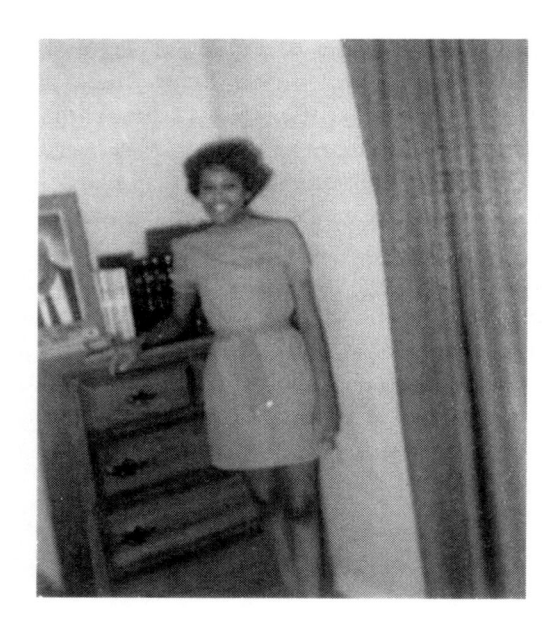

Velma and I lived in my apartment until she reported to Thomasville, Georgia, to become an English teacher. I stayed with her for two weeks in Thomasville until my departure day. She drove me to the Atlanta airport for the first leg of my return to the Philippines just as Gen. MacArthur had done during WW II.

Once I arrived at Clark Air Base, I was assigned to Construction Management Division of the 6200 Civil Engineering Squadron. My job was to inspect military contracts and to ensure the accuracy of the work. My job ran from janitorial services to construction of entire buildings and all contracts in between. I felt good about being assigned to this division because only the top civil engineering personnel get this opportunity.

My supervisor was the best person ever to be in a uniform, SSgt. Sidney Kula. He was born and raised in Hawaii. SSgt. Kula was a firm believer in upward mobility. He would allow his subordinates time to study the Weighted Airman Promotion System (WAPS) test. When I received a line number for Staff Sergeant (E-5), SSgt. Kula immediately directed me to send for my seven level CDCs for 55270. There are 0, 3, 5, 7, and 9 levels in the CDC system. In order to be awarded the 7th level, a person must also be in a 7th level position on the manning chart. Construction Management had only one 7th level slot and SSgt. Kula occupied that position. However, being true to his beliefs, he stepped down and put me on the 7th level position. On paper SSgt. Kula worked for me. In the office everybody knew SSgt. Kula was the NCOIC of Construction Management.

As a NCO (E-5), I was also allowed to live off base. I moved into a house in Marisol Village. This housing development was in Angeles City. SSgt. Robinson and I shared the expenses. We hired a young lady to take care of the house and our clothes. Robby and I split the cooking duties. The great thing about our partnership was that Robby owned a car. When he was working, I could use his car to run the streets and take care of business.

Robby bought a new Honda 750 motorcycle. I had learned to ride a Honda 90. Naturally, I thought I was good, so I asked Robby if I could take his new bike around the block. I took off on this big Honda 750. Everything was going great until Marisol Minor Hotel jumped out in front of me. All I could think was SSgt. Robinson was going to kill me for wrecking his brand new Honda 750. I have not ridden a motorcycle since that damn hotel episode.

January 22, 1970, was my reenlistment date. I could not wait to re-up because of the bonus but mostly because of the thirty days and priority status on flights to the USA. By relisting, I would be able to visit my new wife in Thomasville, Georgia. I requested a forty-day vacation, so I could fly over Vietnam to Thailand in order to get my bonus tax free. That week in Thailand was so good. I spent my bonus and had to return to the Philippines to get more money. Luckily for me, I had many rich Filipino friends from years past. My priority flight status was still good based on my leave orders. I flew to Travis AFB, California, and took another hop to Robins AFB, Georgia. Within twenty-four hours, I was in Thomasville with my green-eyed Angel, Velma. She shared a house with two college roommates, Barbara and Martha. The only difference was they were not married. I had been home for a week when

I began to notice strange events. Velma had told me she had a part-time job reading and editing a newspaper for one Mr. Inman.

Well, I observed that often Velma would answer the phone and say, "She is not home." Several times both Barbara and Martha were home. This began to bother me so one day I decided to search the house. I found a Christmas gift list. There were several names but one name was listed three times. Everyone else including me were listed only once. I thought that strange. A few days later, the phone rang and Velma answered in the kitchen and I picked up in the bedroom. The male voice on the line said, "Can you talk?" Velma responded, "I am sorry, she is not home." The man again said, "Can you talk?" Velma again said, "She is not home" and hung up the. I went into the kitchen to confront my green eyed angel. I asked, "Who was that on the phone?" Velma said, "Oh! It was for Martha." I got mad and hurt at the same time. My wife had gone from a green—eyed angel to a lying bitch. I slapped Velma with all my strength. I wanted to kill her.

All I could do was cry. I called my mother, and she told me not to hurt Velma but get in my car and come home. As I drove down the highway with tears running down my face, all I could think about was going back and killing Velma, my green-eyed devil. I drove past a Catholic Church and decided to stop and talk to the priest. That was the best decision I ever made. The priest calmed me down. We talked for a long time. He agreed that going home was a good idea to get away from a bad situation.

When I am angry, I cook to calm myself down. With cooking in mind I stopped by a large food store to buy some items to cook when I got to Macon. Each time I thought about Velma, it made me cry. I cried as I walked through the store. A kind middle-aged lady noticed me crying.

She thought there had been a death in my family. I explained my situation to her and told her that I wanted to kill my wife. She knew I was serious so she invited me to back to school with her where she worked as a secretary. The name of the school was Oclockney Elementary. I forgot the lady's name over the years. However, it was that lady that really talked me out of killing my wife. She asked me "Do you love your wife?" Then she said, "If you do, then you have to forgive her. After all, you left her in bad company with two young single women." She said, "If I were you, I would go back to Thomasville and get her, take her on a trip out of town, and renew the love I have for her." I called Velma from the school phone. I told her to pack some clothes for a few days.

Velma and I went to Silver Spring, Florida. We talked and did a lot of fun-filled things. We visited a rattlesnake and alligator farm. Velma even took pictures of herself holding a snake. I still had not forgiven her for cheating on me, but I didn't want a divorce, nor go to jail for murder.

After two days in Florida, my love for Velma took over. I tried my best to get her pregnant. In fact, I spent the rest of my vacation working on ensuring that I was successful in starting my first child. When we returned home, Velma promised me that the relationship with Mr. Inman was over. I called Mr. Inman, and I told him if I ever heard that he had been talking to my wife again, I was going to tell his wife and then kill his black ass. My leave ended, and I had to return to the PI. No, I am not naive enough to believe that Velma stopped seeing that man in Thomasville. I am sure her roommates told him exactly when I was to leave home. I am sure it was business as usual five minutes after I boarded that C-130 aircraft bound for Nam with a stop in the Clark Air Base, Philippine Islands.

I lost a lot of respect for my wife from that bad experience. My return to the PI gave me a new outlook on life. Before the Velma/Inman situation, I was true to my wife. When I got back to the Philippines, I went buck wild. I had women for breakfast, lunch, and dinner. That was the only way to keep my mind occupied and away another man banging my wife. Exactly one month after returning to the PI, I called Velma. The first thing she told me was, "James, I love you." The next thing she said was, "My period came this morning." That meant we had wasted twenty-five days of raw sex. My only hope now was for the next five months to pass so my wife could join me in the Philippines.

The situation that made me want to kill my wife was nothing new. Each and every day, a military person has some problem or the other in their marriage. There are many Mr. Inmans in the world. They prey on lonely wives. This just goes to prove that when the military separates families the military members can expect the powers that be to say, "SHIT."

The monsoon season starts in April. During the monsoon season, it rains every day. There are floods everywhere during this time of the year. Many snakes leave their hiding places and just float down the streets. But even these snakes do not stop the military men and women from partying. All we did was to put on combat boots and do what we do. The clubs place the jukeboxes on soda crates and play the music as loud as ever. The service personnel dance and drink as usual.

The PI is noted for a drink known as "Shakem Up." It is a blend of PI Gin and pineapple juice. This concoction will really shake you up if you drink enough (two glasses). The girls that work in the clubs get paid by the number of drinks they can talk the GI into buying them. The drinks the girls were having was just watered-down coke. The girls could also be sex partners for a price. The Philippines was a heaven to men bound for Vietnam. The girls were beautiful and ready to please your every need.

Velma's orders to join me in the PI finally arrived. She was to travel during the month of June, 1970. In May, I received a phone call from Velma. She had been in a bad car accident. She totaled my car but by the "Grace of God" she did not get a scratch. She was highly upset because she knew I was crazy about my cougar. What she didn't know was that though, I was crazy about the car I was in love with her. I had been engaged thrice, but she was the one I married.

I told her not to worry about the car. I would have my mom take care of the car. I told Velma to contact the people at Robins AFB, Georgia. They would direct her travel and shipment of household goods from Thomasville to Clark Air Base, Philippine Islands.

I called my mother and stepfather. I told them to go to Thomasville and tow my car back to Macon. My stepfather owned an old ford that needed an engine. I told him to remove the 289 engine from my car and put it in his ford. He had my permission to junk the rest. A few weeks later, I called home and my mother told me that they had gone to get the car. However, after a test drive around the block a couple of times, they drove it home. Mom said the cougar had a big ugly dent on the passenger side but it drove great. I sent my parents "power of attorney" with instructions to ship my beat up cougar to me in the Philippines.

While waiting for Velma to arrive, I found a house for us. Our house was located on Third Street in Marisol Village. The house was fenced-in with three bedrooms, two bathrooms, a living room, kitchen, and a washroom. The house was going to need a maid and a yard person. These two are luxuries but are considered a necessity in military households in the PI.

Two months later, my ugly cougar landed in the PI. I had already made arrangements with a local repair shop to fix my baby. A friend of mind working in the aircraft paint shop gave me two gallons of blue paint. In the PI, car dents are repaired by removing the affected area and then beating out every dent. After two months, Velma and I had a new sky-blue cougar.

S.H.I.T—Servicemen Have It Tough

On the day Velma arrived, fortunately, I had borrowed a car from one of my friends, so we had transportation from the base to the house. The base provided furniture for the house.

Naturally, I had acquired many friends during my two tours in the Philippines.

I am sure you remember Sandy Thomas from my first tours. Well, he spent a tour in Nam with another Red Horse unit that had disbanded and the majority of the personnel were sent to 5th Tactical Control Group at Clark Air Base, PI. Due to friendship with Sandy, I was introduced to new friends who were crazy as hell in a nice fun-filled way. This new group of friends loved playing practical jokes. I told them that my new wife was not accustomed to dealing with military personnel. I also told them that she did not drink alcohol or curse. SSgt. Robert Marshall from Tennessee said that in less than a year, he would have Velma call me a bitch. Sandy, Marshall, and Roy Walker were like the three stooges, Curly, Moe, and Larry. There was one other, my co-worker, Edwin Matthews, from Alabama, who was such a fool. We were a very tight group of Red Horse-trained men.

I tried everything I could to keep Velma's arrival a secret. Somehow, the tight group knew not only the date but the exact time. They were all at the terminal waiting for me to greet my wife. The minute I kissed the woman, their practical jokes started.

Velma was just like me at the pot-party in LA, green as a pool table and twice as square. The Stooges first started with statements just loud enough for Velma to hear. "Why does James see other women when his wife is so beautiful?" "I see why he put that young girl out." "How is he going to explain that woman's car in their driveway?" Each one of those fools took turns at introducing themselves and whispering statements. It was like a motorcade going to my house. When we got to the house, Marshall said, "Mule, I thought you gave that car back to that woman." He knew damn well that the car belonged to Robby. All I could do was laugh. The expression on Velma's face told me she didn't think it was a joke. Those four idiots had even spent money to have a sign carved saying, "Welcome Home, Mule & Festus." Once Velma got over the shock, they then presented Velma with beautiful housewarming gifts. Oh! The names "Mule and Festus" is from the old Gunsmoke television series. The group started calling me "Mule" in the fall of 1969, when I played football for the 6200th Green Hornets. According to the fools on kickoff, I ran down the field like a mule. Of course, in the show Festus owned the mule so it was a more appropriate nickname for Velma. Now, more than forty years later, my name is still Mule and Festus was Velma's name until her death in 2003.

I did 90 percent of the cooking for Velma, the house girl/maid, and myself. By the way, my first house girl's name was Philly. She looked and acted just like Olive Oil in the Popeye cartoon.

I could have gotten a far better-looking maid, but I didn't want Velma to be intimidated by another pretty woman in her house. In a very short period of time, they became road dogs.

Philly even tried to teach Velma how to cook. One day, I came home and my sweet wife had prepared me dinner. The two of them had cooked fried chicken, mashed potatoes and gravy, green beans, and biscuits. The meal was great with the exception of the biscuits. Those biscuits were so hard that when I threw one in the trashcan, it made a dent the size of the one my baby had put in my cougar. She had forgotten to put baking powder in the mixture. I did not mean to hurt my baby's feeling, but I did. She didn't try cooking for over six months after that incident.

However, with Philly's help, she learned to love most of the Philippines food. Both would clean the house, go clothes-shopping, and to restaurants. When she found a clothing item she wanted, she would buy cloth and have it made. She hired a seamstress one-day-a-week to make her clothes. Velma was living the high life.

One afternoon, a gentleman stopped by the house and wanted to know when we were moving out of his house. The old landlord had sold the house without informing me. We were given one week to vacate the house. I delegated that job to Velma and she recruited Philly. In two days, they had found a house that she was happy with. The new house was larger and cheaper. I really didn't care as long as she was happy. I was tickled pink. The entire gang came to help us move into the new house.

A week later, Sandy and Walker invited all of us to their house for red beans and rice, along with barbeque ribs, and cornbread. The meal was great. I told the group that the next week would be my treat because I had a huge hambone that I had been saving for just such a feast. Well, the three stooges started laughing all at once. The joke was on me. When they were helping Velma and me move, they stole my hambone and cooked the beans we had just eaten.

For Christmas, we gave one another gag gifts. For instance, I gave Marshall a dogfood bowl in which he demanded to be fed Christmas dinner. We gave Marshall's wife Lorraine a toilet seat stool to replace the broken one in the guest toilet. Well, I forgot what they gave Velma but they gave me a 24"× 24" gift-wrapped box with three prophylactics. During the move, Sandy stole one of the rubbers along with my hambone. A week later, he came by the house and asked Velma to give him one of the rubbers so he could go on the block. He insisted that she get the rubber for him knowing she would notice one was missing. Sandy then said, "Festus, I knew Mule had been cheating." Poor Velma, she fell for their tricks every time. All I could do was hug my wife and reassure her. I had told her many times how military members perpetuate SHIT.

One evening, I decided to go on the strip and hang out with the fellows. Velma said I could not go. I was determined to go. I got into the car and started the engine, when Velma came outside with a large kitchen knife. She proceeded to stab both front tires. When she realized how angry I was, she said, "I didn't mean to let all the air out." All I could do was laugh and go to bed.

We worked hard during the week. On the weekend, the crew went to different houses. The best cook of all was Carolyn Burris. That sister could throw down in the kitchen. Now, MSgt Elbert Burris could throw down the whiskey. He would say, "Give me a piece of liquor." A piece of liquor was a 12 oz. tea glass of Old Grand Dad Whiskey. Whenever we went to the Burris's house, we were in for a treat of Carolyn's cooking and a weekend of double-deck pinochle card games. Carolyn would cook enough food to feed an army.

The longer we played pinochle, the more the ladies regretted leaving. We eventually had to teach them how to play the game. After a few outings, the ladies were challenging the men. This was okay, except the men no longer had an excuse to stay out all night playing cards.

The summer went by too quickly. I was only a sergeant (E-4) and money was short. Velma went looking for work. She got a substitute teaching job at a junior high school. Everything was going great now that we had more money coming in. Thanksgiving in 1970 brought me more than a turkey. I had waited two years for my wife to say, "James, I am pregnant." The ironic thing was within two weeks Lorraine and Carolyn also announced their pregnancies. Those three ladies were so cute when they were pregnant. Each one had a seamstress make their maternity clothes. They almost never wore the same maternity smock twice.

One day, SSgt Kula asked if I would go to Taipei in Taiwan, with him to find an air conditioning unit. Of course I said yes because that was a part of

China, and I had never been to China. We could not find the AC unit, so we used the rest of our time buying baseball equipment and baby clothes. SSgt Kula and I did a lot of sightseeing while Taipei.

When I returned to the Philippines with a luggage full of boy baby clothes, Velma thought I was crazy. She asked me what if the baby was a girl. I told her if the baby was a girl I would send her back. Well, on August 10, 1971, Velma gave birth to a bouncing baby boy. Christopher Michael Wimes was the only baby boy born that entire week. He was not the largest baby weighing just 10 lbs and 8oz. A girl was born the same day, weighing 14 lbs and 13 oz to a mother who weighed about 100 lbs.

Velma was awarded two great gifts in August 1971. One, she gave birth to Chris, and two, DODDS (Department of Defense Dependent Schools) gave her a permanent job as a special education teacher. She was assigned to teach a PSA (Personal Social Adjustment) class. PSA was the forerunner of Behavior Disorder (BD). She held that job for two years. She spent each summer on a task force to design other areas of special education. Clark Air Base was one of the very few assignments that a military family could be assigned to regardless of their child's disability. Her assignment to the task force was due in part to Velma's work in the area of special-needs children.

It was during Velma's pregnancy that I met a doll in the Philippines. One Sunday morning, Velma insisted that I go get her some captain wafers. She and Philly had bought these cookies on one of their shopping sprees. I had no idea where to find these cookies. I took the car to go find what my baby wanted. When I got to the entrance-way of the housing compound, there stood this beautiful Pilipino girl. Her hair reached the calves of her gorgeous legs. I asked her where I could these cookies. She directed me to the market area. "Where is that?" I asked. She smiled and said, "If you will give me a ride to church, I will show you." The ride took about twenty minutes. During that short trip, she and I developed a lifelong bond. We exchanged our work telephone numbers. She was a student at Holy Angel College and worked for the electric company. Her name was Esmilita Templug. I asked if I could shorten her name and call her Esther. Again she smiled and said okay. She and I became very close. I even let use my use my address to get letters from her boyfriend, Mr. Bryant Wallace of Washington, DC I didn't know he was her boyfriend until I accidently opened a letter that was returned to me from the States. In the letter, she had talked about their wedding day. Although I really cared for Esther, there was little I could say. I had a wife and a baby was on the way.

S.H.I.T—Servicemen Have It Tough

I confronted Esther. She explained that she hadn't wanted me to know for fear I would not let her use my mailbox to get letters from Bryant. She and I talked every day. Some evenings, I picked her up from work. She was such a sweet young lady. Her biggest thrill was to ride to the big US air base and buy some Neapolitan ice cream and glazed donuts. The more we saw of one another, the closer we got. I would take her on trips with me throughout the Philippines to play tennis I would even take her on temporary duty trips to different bases. She felt like a princess. Even though we were very close friends, Esther was true to Bryant and kept me true to Velma. She would always say that she was saving her virginity for the man she marries.

One day, Esther called me and she was crying. She told me that Bryant was coming to take her as his wife. He had asked her to marry him the very first time he saw her, which was also the last time. She was that attractive. She asked for my opinion as to whether she should get married. By that time, I was too close to the situation to give an unbiased opinion.

I told Esther that the PI was a hard place to live. If she were given the opportunity to leave, she should take it. After all, I now have a wife and a son. If we ever hope to see one another again it would have to be in the USA. She agreed but said that she wanted me to meet Bryant and she wanted to meet Velma. Yes, I thought she was out her ever-loving mind. However, once she explained her thoughts, it all made sense. She said if we were true friends our spouses should know each other. This way we could visit each other in Washington, DC.

Two weeks later, Bryant Wallace arrived in the Philippines. He and Esmilita Templug became Mr. and Mrs. Bryant Wallace. After their honeymoon, Mr. and Mrs. Wallace were invited to my house for a soul food dinner of greens, potato salad, corn bread, BBQ ribs and chicken, and pound cake with ice cream. We had a great time. A week later, Esther and her new husband left the PI for a new life in Washington, DC.

My best friend and traveling companion was gone. I was truly happy for both of them. Esther still used my mailbox to write me and her family. She even called me once a month. Bryant now was proven SHIT.

Fall is the best time of year in the Philippines. There is little rain, and the temperature is moderate. It is also the football season. The old mule was back on the field. I played noseguard at 208 lbs. There were two big tackles on either side of me. William Colbert and Hariam Walker weighed 265 and 285 lbs. At that time, the air force had no AFR. 39-11 (Weight Program). I bet that was due to the Vietnam War. That year, we won the base championship. The 6200th Combat Support Group Green Hornets were awarded a trip to the Turkey Bowl in Manila, the capital of the Philippines. The Turkey Bowl pitted the air force against San Miguel Naval Station. The wing commander flew the team and their families to the game on his C-118 aircraft.

The halftime show was a pushball game between two Filipino teams. Pushball is a game played with a gigantic ball about 10 feet in diameter and eleven men teams. The object of the game is to push this big ball to goals on each end of the field. The game is hilarious with bodies flying everywhere. There is only one rule: Do whatever you can to get that big ball to your goal, whatever you can. Pushball is a game whereby our personnel could not use the excuse of SHIT.

After the football season ended, I was bored. I decided to enroll in college again at the University of the Philippines (UP). I remember only two professors, Dr. and Dr. Ventura. The male Dr. Ventura taught Management I for which I received an "A." The female Dr. Ventura taught American Foreign Policies for which I received an "F." That woman gave me the only "F" I received in six college degrees. She had studied at Michigan State University, and I flatly refused to accept her way of thinking. The USA is the greatest country in the world, but she would allow discrimination to exist. I attended UP through the summer of 1972.

By August of 1972, Christopher had been walking for two months. He was then weighing a whopping 36 lbs. He ate like a horse. In fact, Christopher ate so much that the merchandise control office started an investigation. They thought I was black marketing baby food. However, when I presented Chris to them, the case was closed. My son had been exposed to SHIT.

I had received my next assignment notification in June 1972. My family and I were returning to Eglin Air Force Base, Florida, the same place that I received my Red Horse training four years prior. This time, I was assigned to the main base instead of Field Three, that hole in the woods. Florida is a beautiful place. The white sandy beaches of Fort Walton Beach are spectacular. During the winter time, when the temperature drops to freezing, the sand felt like snow.

I was put in as a base civil engineer on the Structural Maintenance and Repair Team (SMART). This was the only job open for a carpenter. As a staff sergeant (E-5), I was put in charge of a crew of five airmen, each crew comprising two carpenters, one plumber, painter, and an electrician.

At first, I did not like the job. However, as I began to know my crew and learn their jobs, the more fun it became. The job also saved me a lot of money as a homeowner later in life.

At the first opportunity, I made an appointment to see the commander. I was told he was the only person authorized to allow me time to attend college, especially during duty hours. I wanted an extended lunch period, thirty minutes on both sides of 1200 hours, so I could attend Okaloosa-Walton Junior College (OWJC). The thirty minutes was so I could get to class and get back to work after class.

The one thing that made OWJC meaningful was the one professor I remember most. Dr. George Castle was an old man that was very well dressed. He was also the driving force in my majoring in social studies. Dr. Castle taught world history so well that no student ever missed his class because to do so meant missing out on an hour of laughter. One day, Uncle Sam caused me to miss Dr. Castle's class, so I had a classmate record the lecture. That night, I was transcribing the notes and was laughing so loud that Velma thought I was playing a Richard Pryor album. His class also helped me lose about 30 lbs because that semester I did not eat lunch in the Mess Hall.

One weekend, the family and I drove to Georgia to visit relatives. We no sooner got to Macon when Velma decided she needed some items from Walmart. As we drove into the parking lot, a dumb blonde cut across the lot and hit my new 1973 Grand Prix head on. The impact threw Velma into the windshield. Luckily, Chris was in his car seat in the rear seat. Velma sustained a concussion and was sent to the hospital. Neither my son nor I was, but, on the other hand, my car was wiped out.

Now it was time for me to talk to that foolish woman. Naturally, she said it was my fault because I was driving too fast. I called her a stupid female dog but not in those words. The police came but could not write a ticket for fault because we were on private property. I had insurance, so I didn't care. That fool had only insurance to cover her car, not liability as required by law. It would take almost seven years to settle this case. My insurance company paid to have my car completely restored. It would take almost seven years to settle this case due to my being assigned overseas.

After several weeks, my car was returned as good as new. My friend, CM.Sgt. (E-9) J. C. Camper and I went to Atlanta to see Hank Aaron hit the famous 715th home run, thus passing Babe Ruth. While on the way to Atlanta, we stopped in Macon, Georgia, to visit my mother and sisters. That was a mistake. Another woman hit my car again. We never made it to the game. We drove the wrecked 1973 Gran Prix back to Florida with the front end wired up with clothes hangers. That Monday, I took the unlucky car to the first General Motors Dealership and traded it for a new Olds Toronado. As usual, the car dealer was preparing to rip me off. The dealer offered me a $5,000 trade-in. I accepted the offer without any discussions because I only paid $4,500 at the Base Exchange. The new Olds was fully equipped for $7,995. Velma was now working and agreed to help pay for the Toronado.

We needed two cars, so I went to the base salvage yard to an auction. I bought a 1968 Olds for $44. The car had been abandoned on base, and there were no keys. I towed the car home. One day, I decided to see if the car would start. I straight-wired the ignition, and to my surprise, the Olds fired right up. With new tires, gas, and oil, I drove that car for three years. When I got orders for Sembach Air Base, Germany, the 1968 Olds was sold to my sister for a whopping $44. Sandra was a benefactor of SHIT.

During the summer of 1974, Velma and I packed up all our household goods and shipped them to Germany. This way, when we got there in August, all we had to do was find a house. Velma and Chris went to spend the summer in Reynolds, Georgia, with Savannah and James Lockhart. I moved into the barrack until my shipment date.

I took only two weeks' leave along with four days' travel time. My point of departure was Charlton AFB, South Carolina. My last night was spent visiting friends and family. Ms. Carolyn Jackson grew up with the Appling family the same as did I. Daisy Appling took in all children that attended Appling High School.

Before I got married to Velma, I was crazy about Carolyn. Little did I know that when Carolyn was a student at Spelman College in Atlanta, she was going with Richard Appling. There were times I would drive to Atlanta to pick up Carolyn and then drive to Albany State College so she could spend time with Richard. Dorothy and I were fooled by both of them. In fact, Carolyn got pregnant by Richard while in college. She lied about the father of her baby for three years. She finally told me the truth on my last night in Georgia. I went home to get some rest before my family and I departed for Germany.

The next morning, Velma, Chris, and I left Macon for Charlton, South Carolina. Velma was driving while I was trying to catch up on my sleep. Velma awakened me in the middle of the bridge between Georgia and South Carolina. The bridge is elevated more than 100 feet above the river. When she noticed the height of the bridge, she wanted me to take the wheel of the car in the middle of the bridge. The only problem was there was no place to pull over. Therefore, I enthusiastically told her not to stop on the bridge because we may get hit by another vehicle. We made it safely across the bridge. The next day, my car was shipped from Charlton Harbor. The next morning, we boarded a plane for Frankfurt, Germany.

The flight across the Atlantic Ocean for the first five hours was going fine. All of a sudden, I thought I was about to die. A pain hit me in the chest like a bolt of lightning. The female flight attendant asked, "Is there a doctor on the plane?" The pain lasted about 10 minutes with the doctor working on me. When I got to Frankfurt, my friends, Carolyn and Elbert Burris, were waiting for us. The Burris family was with us in Macon and the Philippines. Well, they were now assigned to Wiesbaden AB, Germany. This was July 2, 1974.

They rushed me to the largest military hospital in Europe, Wiesbaden Medical Center. I stayed in the hospital for two days. The doctors and machines could not determine what had happened to me on the plane. In fact, I was given a complete physical examination before I was discharged from the medical center. On July 4, 1974, Burris picked me up and took me to their house where Velma and Chris stayed while I was in the hospital. The ironic thing that also happened was the Burris and Wimes' families watched the Fourth of July fireworks at Wiesbaden AB in a snowstorm. I had never been that cold in December, not to mention July. The next day, I was given the all clear to continue my trip to Sembach Air Base, Germany.

We arrived at Sembach Air Base and checked into the billeting office. That Monday, I went to the housing office for a list of vacant housing in the area. I found a house in Sembach Village. Velma loved the little two-bedroom house. It was close to the base. The only drawback to the house we did not know was the German landlords did not turn on the heat until October. The coldness of Wiesbaden followed us to Sembach. My seven days in processing time ended, and I had to start working. The base delivered base furniture, and

TMO (Traffic Management Office) delivered my personal furniture from the States at the same time.

The fortunate thing I did was to go to football practice the day before. I met some great and kind men. There was one named S. Sgt. Montgomery. He gave me his extra car to use until mine arrived from the United States. Needless to say I took him up on his offer. As the workers were putting the furniture in the house, I noticed that Christopher was having what appeared to be a seizure. His eyes had rolled back in his head. I grabbed my son and drove as fast as I could to Landstuhl Medical Center. Chris was coming around as we arrived at the ER. The medical staff took over and admitted Chris. He stayed in the hospital for four days while they conducted test after test. The doctors could not identify the cause for his seizures.

The change in weather almost killed my son. August and September were very warm months. October was even pleasant. November came, and it started to get cold again. However, everything was fine because I had made friends, and my family was warm and healthy.
Chris and Velma no longer had to spend most of the day in bed and the rest of the day in the kitchen with the oven door open to keep warm.

My car arrived in early September. I took a bus to Bremerhaven, West Germany, on the North Sea. I retrieved my big beautiful 1973 Toronado Olds. I drove sensibly for fifty miles from Bremerhaven to Bermen to give the car a chance to lubricate itself. Berman is where the autobahn starts south. I set the cruise control on 110 mph. European cars were passing me as if I were standing still. The autobahns have four lines of traffic from right to left. The first right lane is for Volkswagens and American cars. The second lane is for midsize German and French cars. The third lane is for large engine French, German, and Italian cars. The fourth lane is for fools with a death wish by driving above 130 mph. I pulled my Olds in the first lane so I could drive a very slow 90 mph and live to enjoy my SHIT.

After just four months in Sembach Village, the Wimes family was offered a house in Vogelweh Military Housing in Kaiserslautern. I quickly accepted the house at 1116 L Vogelweh. After all, military housing was cheaper, plus all the heat was controlled in each individual unit. Velma was also happy because as soon as we moved into the house, she applied for a job at Vogelweh High School. She could not get a teaching position, but they did offer her a job as a teacher's aide in a special needs class. With our need for money, Velma readily accepted the position. The high school was a short walk from the house.

Whenever she needed our car, I would catch a ride to Sembach Air Base with S.Sgt. McDonald or Montgomery.

Sports composition in Europe among military bases is like sports between colleges in the States.

I played football during the winter and tennis all day and half the night during summer. Germany is a small country in land area. Therefore, to travel from base to base to support your team was one of the perks to see the entire country. One weekend, we went to Rhein-Main Air Base for a football doubleheader. The Sembach Air Base Tigers were playing the Hahn AB Hawks. As usual, the Burris family agreed to meet us in Frankfurt. This way, Velma and Chris would have company while I played on the field. During the game, Chris and Kevin would just play.

There was one play whereby an old friend from the Philippines (A1C Hunt), weighing about a "buck 05," hit me at the knees and stood me on my head. I just knew he was going to move but he didn't. When I regained my senses, all I could say was, "Get me up so I can kill him." He had made a great play, but he stood over me bragging, "I got me one. I got me one." Hunt's coach took him out of the game because he heard me threaten to kill him. We won the game by some outrageous score. After the game, we had dinner at the NCO Club with our extended family before heading back to Kaiserslautern, West Germany.

Chris almost never watched the games. He would go to play and eat junk food. The one play that almost killed me, he was watching. On the way home, he was in the backseat and said to me, "Dad, you got two holes in your head (bald spots)." He then said, "Dad, I saw you lying on that field playing dead." All I could do was laugh and think that military dependents know SHIT.

That next summer was very hot in Germany. It was so hot I installed an air conditioner in my house. We had the only air conditioner in all of Vogelweh Housing. When I was not at work, I could be found on the tennis courts. During the summer months in Germany, I could play tennis without lights until 2300 hours. On the weekends, we played for thirteen or fourteen hours. My usual tennis partner was one of the base chaplains. Capt. Jamison would leave the courts on Sunday morning, go take a shower, cover himself in a robe, preach morning services, and be back on the court before he was missed. On Saturday evening, Velma and Mrs. Jamison brought our dinner to the court. They said the next thing they were bringing was our clothes. My playing tennis paid off, for I won the Sembach Air Base Tennis tournament. The winner received a slot in the United States. Armed Forces Europe (USAFE) tournament held in Munich, West Germany. This was an all-expenses-paid vacation in the Bavarian Alps for a week. Bavaria is the prettiest area of Germany, especially with its snow-capped peaks in the summertime. It was during that tournament that I realized tennis is an elitist sport. There were only two blacks from all European Military Complexes playing in this tournament. We were celebrities. Everyone came out to see the black man from Holland and the black man from Germany.

One day, while he and I were practicing, I noticed a young lady standing by the fence just watching our every move. We took a break; so I went over to introduce myself. She told me her name was Koloma and that her family was from Kazakhstan, Russia. During our conversation, she told me that she was visiting her father at the language academy. He taught Russian to American Military Personnel. She spoke very good English. While we talked, she told me that she had heard there were two blacks playing in the tournament, and she had never seen a live black man. At that point, I invited her to see us play the next day at the Munich Tennis Club. She was so excited.

My match was scheduled for 11:00 a.m., so I picked her up about 10:00 a.m. Her father answered the door. He was a big Russian with a very deep voice. He was also very concerned about his daughter. He asked many questions while I waited for Koloma to get dressed. She was a beautiful twenty-three-year-old college student. She was belle of the ball, so to speak. If it had not been for our special guest, the last day of the tournament was a complete bust. I lost in straight sets (6-2/6-2), and my friend also lost in straight sets (6-4/6-3). At the awards banquet, I did receive the best-dressed man award. Oh yes, I was clean with everything matching but my tennis game. The highlight of the trip was being able to cross the Alps Mountain as Hannibal had done around 180 BC.

Bavaria is one of the prettiest places on earth, especially with snow-capped mountains even in the summertime. The tennis week was over, and I had packed to return to Kaiserslautern. The last thing I did was a visit to Koloma and her family. She and I exchanged coins as a lasting friendship. She gave me a Russian Ruble, and I gave her a silver dollar. As I headed my car north, all that was on my mind was Velma and Chris. They were waiting for me with open arms and open hands for their souvenirs. The one souvenir I brought home was an authentic CoCo Clock for which Bavaria is noted.

The summer in 1975 turned into winter. Football season was now opened. There was only one difference—Montgomery and McDaniels were being transferred back Stateside. I was losing two of my best friends. The good thing was Velma was offered a full-time teaching position in the same class where she had been an aide the previous school year. She had no special education credential; her principal said it was okay because he knew who taught the class the year before.

We now needed two cars. McDaniels had ordered a new car and wanted to sell his 1965 Ford Mustang for $500. It was a blessing in disguise. I gave Velma the GasHog, and I took the little pony. We were quite satisfied until the Office of Special Investigation (OSI) called me in for an interview. They wanted to know how I could afford a new Oldsmobile and a Ford Mustang in Germany on an E-5 pay. I almost got arrested for insubordination for cursing a superior.

I told them if they had conducted a proper investigation, they would have discovered that my wife made more money than the O-5 that signed the orders to investigate me in the first place. Needless to say, the OSI agent felt stupid particularly when they called civilian personnel office for her salary.

Germany is a beautiful country. Sembach Air Base was located on a hill overlooking Sembach Village. My job was again in Construction Management, monitoring contracts for USAF. I truly enjoyed my job. Col. Wheat, a black O-5, was the unit commander. He was a fair person when it came to discipline. One day, he called in for a counseling session (ass chewing). He was upset with me because I had borrowed $250 from a contractor. This was a conflict of interest because I was the inspector of her janitor contract. However, at the time, I borrowed the money I had been reassigned to the carpenter shop. Col. Wheat gave me a letter of reprimand (LOR). What saved my stripes? What really saved me was I had repaid the loan. My name surfaced during a major conflict of interest case. An American civilian inspector had threatened the contractor with losing her contract if she did not lend him $5,000. She reported him to the authorities. This started the investigation whereby the civilian was found guilty. He was fired and sent back to the States with his family in disgrace.

Several months passed as I waited for the LOR to be removed from my personnel file. SMSgt. Robert Allen, my friend and neighbor at Vogelweh Housing, was in charge of personnel records.

He called me the day the LOR was to be removed. I went to the personnel office, and he took the LOR out and gave it to me. As minor as a LOR was, it was a major issue to me. This was the first time in thirteen years of military service I had received an official disciplinary action.

Technical Sergeant (E-6) seems like a long way off. I had only four years "time in grade." This was the year for me to get a promotion. The Weighted Airmen Promotion System (WAPS) test was at hand. All I needed to do on the test was well. I did great, but my "time in grade" gave me a high promotion line number. All promotions were spread out over a six-month period. The promotion cycle of 1975 was good because the system allowed too many airmen to get promoted. So instead of six months, I had to wait seven months. It was a struggle for me. I was the only staff sergeant out of ten in the carpenter shop that got a line number for promotion. Oh! Did I forget to mention that I was given every SHIT job at Sembach Air Base? The NCOIC of the wood shop was not to fund of black airmen. He tried everything possible to upset me, so I would do or say something stupid. If I had fallen into his web, my line number would have been red lined (eliminated) from the promotion list.

One week before six months was up, the USAF issued an extension to the wait time. There was a carry over for another month. I could not take another thirty days of mistreatment by this racist man. Then one of my white Red Horse-trained friends told me what the bastard said. He had a meeting with the staff while I was doing one of his dirty jobs. He told them in the meeting that he had thirty days to take my line number. I told my friend I could not take another month of his crap.

The red horseman told me to apply for a thirty-day leave. I did not have thirty days on the book because I sold my leave when I reenlisted several months back. The supervisor said that only the commander could approve a thirty-day leave to the USA. Remember my neighbor, SM.Sgt. Robert Allen; he told me that a reenlistment leave was good for a year. I applied for a reenlistment and Lt. Col. Wheat approved the leave with congratulations on the reenlistment. I went home to pack for my trip to Georgia where I stayed for two weeks. The second two weeks were spent at Vogelweh Housing. At the end of the thirty days, I walked into the carpentry shop as Technical Sergeant James Ellis Wimes. My thanks went to my fellow Red Horseman for his advice.

While in Germany, I met and developed lasting friendships with various military families. My next-door neighbors, Linda and Walter Chester with their four children, were the very weird. First of all, Linda was a religious fanatic. She would cook but would not let the kids eat until late at night when she was sure the preacher wasn't coming. One day, I was off work, so Linda sent her eldest daughter over to ask me for a ride to the commissary. After taking a shower and getting dressed, I went to the car to wait for Linda and the children. I waited for more than an hour before knocking on the door. Linda

S.H.I.T—Servicemen Have It Tough

came to the door and told me that the Lord had told her not to go get the kids some food to eat.

There was another time I gave Linda and the children a ride. However, I decided to get the car washed first. This was a drive through car wash. Once we were inside the car wash and the suds and brushes started their washing actions, the children started screaming and crying and actually trying to get out the car. It was a mess. I never put the Chester family in my car again.

Now through the Chester family, I met Linda and James Baldwin with their two sons. Linda and Velma became the best of friends. James and I became friends and college classmates. For the most part, James and I were babysitters during disco night on base. Linda would come down from the mountains to get Velma for their night out. The two of them were into dancing.

James and I were heavy into college. We took classes at the University of Maryland. One of the highlights of our European College career was a class in Viennese Musical Era. The class was taught in Vienna, Austria. We were allowed to attend the class on TDY orders for two weeks. The lectures were conducted on the bus from Kaiserslautern, Germany, to Vienna. The final exam was conducted on the return trip home. The time in between was spent attending concerts with the Vienna Boys' Choir and the Vienna National Orchestra. We were given time to visit some historical sights such as the training area of the Lipezone Stallions and the home of Sigmund Fraud. The decorations in Fraud's house gave me the idea he was a "freak of the week."

The music halls were designed strictly for classical music. James Baldwin slept through the entire Vienna Boys' Choir concert. However, the music was so great; soothing and sleeping was in order. At one Vienna National Orchestral concert, we were thrilled to the kettledrums sounding out the bombs bursting in air and the trumpets calling the soldiers to battle during their performance of the "1812 Overture." The overall experience was wonderful.

While at the University of Maryland, I took another class that was of great interest to me. The class was "Seminar in Modern Germany." This class really was a comparison of historical and modern Germany. We visited old castles and modern skyscrapers. We visited old vineyards and modern beer breweries. The most exciting part of the class was a cruise on the Rhine River which included a wine-tasting seminar. Life in Germany was wonderful.

Almost daily we met new friends. Willie and Maxine Fields were a couple of friends we ran into at S.Sgt. McDaniels house. S.Sgt. Fields and McDaniels were assigned to the security police section. After talking for a few minutes, we discovered that Maxine was from my hometown of Macon, Georgia. Velma and Linda now had a new running mate, Maxine.

As I said earlier, Velma took a job as a full-time special education teacher. Special needs students in Germany were not allowed to do field trips with regular students. Each year, the special needs students throughout Germany went on a weeklong camping trip during the springtime. We went to the American Boy Scout Camp with the students. Each group required an escort for every four special needs students. I applied to be one of the escorts. My unit commander felt to deny me and would be denying the students.

During the camping trip, they taught the students to repail off the side of a 200 feet cliff. It was a safe endeavor. The worst thing that could happen was for a student to let go all ropes and then turn completely upside down. The trainers set up velour ropes on top and at the foot of the cliff. Either instructor could control or stop the descend of a repailler. Well, to make a long story short, a female student did everything right until she got started off the cliff and let go of the ropes. She turned upside down. Velma and I both almost had a heart attack. The instructors stopped the child in midair and then slowly lowered her to the surface. We knew the student would be devastated. Instead when we rushed to console and comfort her; she jumped up and said, "That was fun. Can I do that again?" Even on camping trips, there was the possibility of SHIT.

My time in Germany was marching on. In fact, time marched me right of Sembach Air Base. The military minds did a restructuring of Germany. The belief that if Germany were to be attacked, the enemy would come from the northeast. The stumbling block would be the Rhine River. Therefore, the vast majority of ground troops should be stationed north of the river, and majority of air force wings were assigned south of the Rhine River.

There were many army bases in the Kaiserslautern area. Naturally, army bases did not measure up to USAF standards. Therefore, a major renovation project was instituted. A prime BEEF team was developed to do the renovation. Yes, I was assigned to the team and was transferred to Ramstein Air Base. This was actually a good move because Ramstein was located in the area of Vogelweh Housing. The transfer placed me fifteen minutes from home as opposed to forty minutes.

If there were a downside it would be my love of football. I could not be assigned to Ramstein and play football for Sembach. The base commander at Sembach wrote a letter to the base commander at Ramstein to get special permission for me to finish the last three games of the season at Sembach. The letter stated that I was a third-string lineman. Well, the game between Sembach and Ramstein Air Bases was the following weekend. During the introduction of the teams, the announcer said, "Starting at nose guard, 6 feet, 220 lbs, from PG. Appling High School of Macon, Georgia, James Wimes."

At that moment, the base commander came to the sideline and whispered in my ear, "I am going to put your ass in jail." That was the first time Sembach defeated Ramstein in ten years. The score was 44-10. I took the game ball over the objections of the NCOIC of the athletics department.

During 1977, I decided to become a Free and Accepted Mason. I went to classes for the first, second, and third degree in masonry. The NCOIC of athletics department was the worshipful master of Ernest W. Lyons Lodge 107 of Free and Accepted Masons. I had completed my third degree to become a master mason and was invited into the consistory. The consistory would elevate me to the 32 degree and the title of Sublime Prince with a crown. I was now able to become a Shiner. However, I had funds only for the consistory. The worshipful master said to me, "If money was the problem, then you don't have a problem." He reached into his pocket and pulled out a wad of money. I told him I was leaving in two weeks and couldn't pay him before I left Germany. He smiled and said, "You are a traveling man now, and you can be trusted by any brother." The Worshipful Master gave me the money to become a Shriner in order to get even with me for that football game. Remember the Ramstein/Sembach game whereby I took the game ball. Well, during my initiation into the Shriners that game ball returned to hunt me. The Potentate hid a football in the temple beat my behind until I found the ball blindfolded. When it was all over, I was presented my fez as a member of Al-Karat Temple of the Mistic Shriners.

My friend and neighbor now, CM.Sgt. Robert Allen had transferred to McConnel AFB, Kansas several months earlier in 1977. I had rented him my mustang when he was out processing. When he returned the car, I bid him a hardy farewell because he would not be seeing his family in Kansas. I was so wrong. When I got my orders, they read 91st Strategic Missile Wing, McConnell AFB, Kansas. By sending me to Kansas, USAF has given me another large helping of SHIT.

Chapter 11

Return to the Sunshine State

    The flight from Germany was uneventful. We flew into Charleston AFB in South Carolina. My car was in port but not off-loaded, so we had to take a bus to Georgia. Three days later, I returned to Charleston for my car. The weather was very hot, so the first thing I checked on the car was the air conditioner. It was not working. I went to the first GMC dealership to get the AC repaired. There was a three-day wait at every dealership for AC repairs. It was at that moment I realized the power of masonry. The white manager of the fourth repair shop was a mason. He said he could not let a brother traveling east nor west drive in that heat. In less than two hours, I was headed to Georgia in AC comfort.

I did not want to go to Kansas. The only thing I knew about Kansas was in the Wizard of Oz. The assignment had to be changed. I made contact with Randolph AFB, Personnel Center and Offutt AFB, Headquarters Strategic Air Command to try to change my assignment to Kansas. I left the family in Georgia with Velma's parents because I was not staying in Kansas. All I could think of in Kansas was Dorothy and Toto. When I got to Kansas, all I could see was miles and miles of wheat fields. It was so depressing. However, when I reached Wichita, Kansas, I was greatly surprised. It was a nice-sized city with more than three hundred thousand in population. McConnell AFB was located five minutes from downtown Wichita. The base was very clean and neat in appearance. The buildings were World War II vintage. I located the billeting office that afternoon and was given a room in the barrack. To elevate my discussion for Kansas, my roommate was an A1C. I being a technical sergeant with an airman for a roommate was an insult.

The following day, I reported to the personnel office to start my in-processing. Yes, you guessed it. The first person to greet me was CM.Sgt. Robert Allen, my friend and neighbor from Sembach Air Base, Germany. He told me that when a copy of my orders was sent to him, he almost passed out laughing at our last day together in Germany. Two days later, it was Thursday, and I was even more depressed. My appetite was nonexistent. My young roommate invited me to go with him to the NCO Club. Thursday was soul night with Disco Granddaddy. At first, I said, "No." Then I decided to see what McConnell had to offer in the way of eye candy. There were more fine women in that club than a man could shake a stick at. I was like the "Spook that Stood By the Door." All I could do was look. Finally, I hit on a fine white lady. She was asked, "May I drive you home." She smiled and walked off. That was not the first time I had been rejected politely. Soul night dance ended at midnight. Again I was standing by the door, when the polite lady walked up and said, "Well, are you going to drive me home or not?"

As I drove to Meridian Housing Area, the young lady and I exchanged information about ourselves. Her name was Sheila. She worked at the NCO Club as a disc jockey. We became friends. The best thing about meeting lady Jade was she changed my mind about McConnell AFB, Kansas. The next day I asked for a leave to go get my family. Velma was called and instructed to pack her and Chris's clothes. We are going to be living in Kansas. The family and I lived in Temporary Housing for two weeks. I found a suitable apartment that was within my financial range. The apartment was a few blocks from the back gate of the base. After about three months, I discovered the neighbors were crazy. One afternoon, I heard a woman arguing with someone. She said, "I am going to shoot the motherfucker in the head because if I shoot him in the ass, it may not kill him." This crazy woman was talking about killing a ten-year-old boy. I went back in the house and told Velma we are moving as soon as possible. The next weekend, we went house hunting.

On October 1, 1977, we found a house at 1919 South Santa Fe. This house was located in a white neighborhood. The house was situated on the backside of the lot. We had a very large front yard and a very small backyard. Velma and I fell in love with the house and closed on October 17, 1977, with the final payment due on October 17, 2007.

Now that we had a house, Velma's next priority was to find a job. Mr. Sam Speight looked at her resume and job application. He said, "We have nothing in English nor music." However, we do have a position in Special Education. Velma took the job in PSA (Personal Social Adjustment).

I had enrolled at Wichita State University (WSU) to complete my requirement for a bachelor degree. During my education in-briefing, the counselor noticed the number of college credits I had. He then offered me the bootstrap program whereby an airman is sent to a college for a year to gain courses to graduate. The only problem was I had only two weeks to get all my paperwork completed. The paperwork included transcripts from all the colleges that I had attended. I knew that was impossible to get transcripts from the University of the Philippines in two weeks. WSU would not give me a letter of acceptance without all transcripts. As I explained that my predicament to the counselor, Mr. Gene Arnenbacker was listening to my every word. Mr. Arnenbacker asked, "If I had considered Kansas Newman College." I had never heard of Kansas Newman College. He went on to explain that it was a private catholic college on the west side of Wichita. He said it was expensive, but my GI Bill would be enough to cover the cost. All I wanted was a letter of acceptance, so I could complete the bootstrap application.

Mr. Arnenbacker took my personal information, and two days later, he returned with a letter of acceptance to Kansas Newman College. We had an agreement that as far as the college was concerned, the letter was unofficial until all transcripts were in. I sent for the transcripts.

The bootstrap application was completed on time and forwarded to Headquarters SAC for approval. I did not expect the application to be approved. Little did I know that McConnell AFB was the number one base in SAC for running education for the last ten years. Well, my application was approved, and I was enrolled at Kansas Newman College as a senior. KNC was a small college with about 750 students of which about a hundred were African Americans.

During my college orientation and transcript evaluation, the counselor noticed that I had as many credit hours in history as I did in government. Sister Roth told me that KNC did not have a major in government but did have a degree in history. Sister Roth continued to explain that if I took three upper level courses in history and a total of thirty hours, KNC could grant me a bachelor degree in history. The University of Maryland required me to get twenty-four hours of anything from an accredited four-year institution, and they would award me a BS degree in government. This decision was a "no brainer"; one degree for twenty-four hours or two degrees for thirty hours. I agreed to take the additional courses, but Sister Roth dropped a bombshell. KNC required six hours of a foreign language. Well, I was back to the twenty-four hours and one degree. After a few minutes, she said that the foreign language requirement can be waived if I have lived in a foreign country for at least a year. I smiled and started naming countries. She and I settled on Germany because I had lived there for the last three years plus I had taken three hours of conversational German. I was now on my way to a two-degree track. This turned out to be the brighter side of SHIT.

As a student at KNC, I was to experience college life for the first time in my life. The USAF was paying the tuition and my salary. All I to do for a year was complete my degree in two semesters. I started at KNC in January 1978. I could attend college in spring and summer or spring and fall semesters. I chose the latter. This meant I had to return to work on base during the summer.

I was given the task of renovating the base chapel so the base commander's daughter's wedding, which was to take place in August 1978. My supervisor was a civilian named Robert M. Walker. Military personnel will always find a shorter and more efficient way of doing a job. The task was to remove 4'×8'×3/4" sheets of plywood from behind the altar and replace it with Sheetrock to comply with the fire codes. Well, one day, Mr. Woods came to the chapel with Maj. Scott. To impress the major, Mr. Woods started shouting at me in a demeaning manner. "Sgt. Wimes, can you read a blue print?" I tried to explain, but he then told me to read the blue printout loud.

Again, I tried to tell Mr. Woods that the blue prints he had were outdated. He would not give me the chance to say anything. He told me to report to the shop and not to return to the chapel. I was fired. I went straight to the major's office. While waiting, Mr. Woods latterly ran past me into the major's office. Knowing the military system, I began to write exactly what the major was going to say to me when I explained my position. Maj. Scott was a man very short in stature with an ego taller than the Statue of Liberty. When the major finished saying exactly what I had written, I requested to see Lt. Col. Black. By that time, I was angry as all hell. I told the secretary that I wanted to see the commander and didn't want to hear anything she had to say.

I went into the commander's office and saluted and started crying at the same time. I said to Col. Black, "If Mr. Woods speaks to me again, I will kill the bastard." The colonel knew I was very serious when he saw this big band black man crying. He told me to go to the orderly room and tell the first sergeant to put me on vacation for a week.

The next week seemed to stand still. When I returned to work, my shop supervisor told me to report to the base commander's office. There was no doubt in my military mind that I was about to lose at least one stripe (reduction of rank) for threatening to kill Mr. Woods. I reported to the base commander with a salute. He told me to be seated while we waited for Lt. Col. Black. When he arrived, the meeting began. The base commander said, "Sgt. Wimes, I have a job for you. Do you play golf?"

I stuck my foot in my mouth and said, "No, I think it is a dumb game."

The base commander responded with, "Well, I am going to send you to the golf course NCOIC of Golf Course Maintenance."

I said, "Sir, I don't know anything about a golf course."

The commander said, "You don't need to have knowledge of the course. I have a civilian at the course with that knowledge, but he doesn't know a damn thing about supervising troops." He then asked if I knew why I was chosen for this job. I said it is because of my supervising skills. He said, "No! It is because Col. Black told me you are the meanest SOB in his unit, and I want someone that knows how to kick ass and take names." Instead of losing a stripe, I became NCOIC of Golf Course Maintenance.

Chapter 12

Coco Clock and Brats

I spent the rest of the summer at the golf course learning how to maintain a quality golf course. The course maintenance equipment was unique and took special training to use properly. For instance, the greens had to be cut less than ¼ inch, the fairways had to be cut to 1", and the roughs had to be cut to 3 inches. Each day, as I conducted my inspections, I would find many different items from golf balls to baby rabbits.

Once I found a baby rabbit that had been abandoned by its mother. The little rabbit was taken home, and it became a family pet. We had a dog named Michael that I will tell about him shortly. Right now, it is Jack, the Rabbit. Jack was raised from 5 ozs to over ten pounds. He got to be too big for his cage. Jack would follow Velma around the house. When Velma became pregnant with our second child, Jack wouldn't leave her side. Whenever we locked Jack in his room, he would scratch like a cat until the door was opened, whereby he headed straight for Velma. Finally, I took Jack, the Rabbit, back to the golf course and set him free.

Now for our first pet named Michael, Michael was a long-haired dachshund dog. Velma got pregnant seven years after Chris was born. One night, she and I were in bed studying for my master sergeant exam. She thought she was sweating and was about to bleed to death.

She had had a miscarriage, so I rushed her to the hospital. All the doctors could do was clean her up because all the damage had been done. Velma had lost Chris's little sister.

We had told Chris that a baby sister was coming, so he would be prepared when the baby was born. That night, Velma stayed in the hospital. I had the task of explaining to Chris that the baby had died, and his mother would be home in a few days. He said if the baby was dead, when was the baby's funeral going to be. He was told there wouldn't be a funeral because the baby was cremated. He did not understand the term cremated. I made the mistake and said the word means to burn up the baby. For the next hour, I had to answer every question of a seven-year-old child could think of about death, funerals, and cremations. Chris finally settled down. He looked me in my eyes and said, "Well, since I can't have a sister, can I have a dog?"

I said, "Yes, Son, you can have a dog."

About two weeks later, I was working my part-time job at the NCO Club as night manager. One of the waitresses came to me crying. When asked why was she crying. She said, "If I tell you, you are going to be mad." Now I was really concerned, so I probed her into telling me. She had brought a dog to work as a gift for her boyfriend who now didn't want the puppy.

The reason I would be angry was because she had hid the dog in the kitchen of the club. If the health inspector had found that dog in the kitchen, I would have been fired for health violations. I went to the kitchen to see this dog and found it was the cutest little puppy. I told the waitress to give me the puppy. After a few minutes of pleading, I convinced her to give me the puppy. The little dog was taken home and presented to Velma. At first sight, she fell in love with the puppy. The next morning, we gave Chris his wish. His face lit up like a Christmas tree. He immediately named the puppy "Michael." When asked why he gave the dog his middle name. My son said, "Well, Dad, if I had gave him my first name, you and Mom may get confused."

My part-time job at the NCO Club was a great in rode to the young ladies. As a night manager of the club, each Thursday, I would meet new people by allowing them entrance to Soul Night with Disco Grand Daddy. Even the college girls were asking me to get them on base for cheap wining and dining in a safe environment. There was not even one fight the entire four years I worked at the club.

During my final semester in college, I met many students from KNC and Friends University. These two colleges were strange because one school represented the Catholic Church and the other school represented the Quaker Faith. A student could be enrolled at either school and was allowed to take any classes from the other. The reason I became associated with students from Friends University was because of the senior level political science courses I needed to graduate.

One of those courses included a trip to the United Nations in New York and the State Department in Washington, DC. There were twelve political science majors and myself on this trip. We had to attend several sessions at the UN. The most memorable session was the debate on the floor between the American and Russian ambassadors over the invasion of Afghanistan by Russia. We were also treated to a Broadway Plays; Whiz starting Stephanie Mills, and For Colored Girl Who Considered Suicide When the Rainbow is Enough. Each night after the plays, as a group, we went to dinner at a famous New York restaurant like Mamma Rosa's Italian Restaurant for pizza and beer. The exception was me being a nondrinker, I had pizza and Pepsi.

The last leg of our trip was to Washington, DC, for a weeklong visit to the Department of State. We arrived in DC on Saturday afternoon. We were given the weekend to visit museums on the mall. On Monday, we started our official visit to the State Department. We were able to meet with Secretary of State Cyrus Vance. However, we were afforded the opportunity for a Q and A session with several of his staff members. Each day, we visited a different venue of the Department of State to observe lectures and discussions. At the end of daily meeting, no Capital Hill our nights were free. We were provided tickets to see the play "1776" at the Ford Theatre.

To me, the highlight of the week was to see the US Marines Corps Band close out the week with a performance on the museum mall. The band played the music of each military branch and ended with the Marine Corps Hymn. When the band played "Wild Blue Yonder" I stood to honor the USAF. Each time I hear those military songs, I tear up because I know SHIT.

Well, it was time to head for Land of Oz, home of Kansas Newman College and Friends University. My undergraduate college career was about to end. As I reflect on the year I spent at KNC, several incidents come to mind. The first was to be called a thief by a nun only because I went into her open door office to put a report on her desk. The thought of what she said took me about thirty minutes to internalize. I walked back across campus and made Sister Thomasine apologize to me.

The second incident was with Sister Deloris. This sweet old lady was the librarian. She had to be the nicest person I had ever met. Once a month, she would say to me, "James, I need a date for lunch. First, we will go to McDonalds for lunch and then you can drive me to the Bible Book Store." This lady was so sweet that she once set up a class during her lunch hour, whereby I was her only student. That class gave me enough credits for an endorsement in language arts.

The third significant incident was with a brilliant young lady named Ann Ducey. Ann was a fine white lady from St. Louis, MO. She only associated with black students. Her boyfriend (Jeff Timony) was a native of Wichita and was one of my best friends. One afternoon, I was sitting in the student center looking sad. Ann came in and asked, "What is your problem?" I told her I had one more paper to write, and my work will be done at Kansas Newman College. She said if you will take me to Soul Night on base, I will help you do your paper. I had completed the research but could not get started writing that paper. I gave Ann all the books and periodicals. Ms. Ducey returned the next day with a rough draft of my research paper. Did I take Ms. Ducey to Soul Night at the NCO Club? You can bet I did and many places thereafter. Even after graduation, she had stayed in touch until she got married and moved away. Jeff and I are still friends. My undergraduate college was over and I was awarded a Bachelor of Science in Government from the University of Maryland. I was also awarded a Bachelor of Art in History from Kansas Newman College. During the fall in 1979, I enrolled as a graduate student at Wichita State University with a major in secondary education. By majoring in secondary education, I could pick all the courses in my graduate program for certification in teacher education.

I started with two media courses because I was working two jobs. All I had to do was watch television each Wednesday night from 6:00 to 8:00 p.m. and write a two-page paper on the program. The class met as a group once a month for four hours to discuss the program, take a short test, and leave. Needless to say, the books we bought had nothing to do with the television shows, so I failed the test every month. The instructor felt sorry for me and gave me two "D's."

WSU was not so sympathetic. The university proceeded to kick me out of grad school which I couldn't afford. I was getting a GI Bill check each month for being in college. I made an appointment to see the dean of students, Dr. James Fisher, about my situation. He instructed me to write a letter to the university requesting probation due to my military status. If I ever used SHIT, it was in that letter. Anyway, the university put me on probation and gave me one semester to pull the 1.0 GPA to a 3.0 GPS. That probationary semester, I made an "A" in one class and a "B" in the second class. That was not enough to pull my GPA to 3.0. I had to write another letter to WSU filled with the SHIT philosophy. I was given one more semester which I made two "A's." Dr. Fisher became my advisor and mentor.

When I was preparing to take my master comprehensive examination, I studied harder than ever before. The white students conducted study sessions weekly for two months. Each week, a couple of the white students would go meet with an instructor to discuss possibilities of test items. At the weekly study sessions, the possible test items would be disseminated to the group. There were eight black students in the secondary education program. However, I was the only one willing to drive forty miles for the study sessions. There was one black female that called the group racist. She took the comps four times that I know of and never passed. I would have met with the KKK if they could have gotten me through the comps.

There was another professor by the name of Dr. Betsy West. Two weeks before the comps test day, Dr. West summoned me to her office for a conference. In her southern drawl (Georgia), she began to explain her concern for me passing the comprehensive examination. She told me my comps will be graded by five university professors. The highest and lowest score will be thrown out and the remaining three scores must equate to a "B." She said she was sure I knew the . . . However, she wanted me to use short and simple sentences because frankly Mr. Wimes you cannot spill worth a damn.

The following Saturday, I took the examination with Dr. West's advice. The exam had only one question with four components, "Design a secondary curriculum for anywhere USA taking into consideration the sociological, economical, and cultural aspect of the area, utilizing an educational theorist philosophy?" I wrote for almost seven hours before completing the exam. I was confident that I had passed the test for my master's degree in secondary education (MEd). After the comps test, I went home to bid Velma and Christopher good-bye before driving to school at Patrick AFB, Florida.

Chapter 13

Defense Equal Opportunity Management Institute

This military school trains all branches of the US Armed Services in the area of equal opportunity and treatment. The name of the school is Defense Equal Opportunity Management Institute (DEOMI). Prior to completing my Med, I had applied to cross-train from civil engineering to EOT. The drive from Kansas to Florida was very long, especially when I had to report on Sunday. I drove all night and all day to get to DEOMI. I was so sleepy that I didn't even remember getting on the Bee Line Expressway.

Once I arrived at the school, I had to make my case for a private room. The rule was Enlisted Grade 6 and below had to share a room. Enlisted Grade

7 and above were given private quarters. I had a line number for promotion to Master Sergeant (E-7) in thirty days. There were five E-7 selectees that were given private rooms.

The first day, I met M.Sgt. Carrie and T.Sgt. Dianne Dalston while in processing. They were to become lifelong friends. The following day, 117 troops took a placement test. This was called the Ops Program. If a person made a high score on the test, you were given the opportunity not go to classes the first two weeks. However, one had to write an article or do a book report. That afternoon, it was announced that only eight individuals received high enough scores to qualify for the Ops Program. I received a reading score of 116 words per minute with a 92 percent comprehension. I was surprised but chose the Ops Program and decided to do a book report for the school's biweekly newspaper. My book report was about the Tuskegee Airmen, *Fighting for the Right to Fight* written by Charles Bacon. The Ops Program was great because when the other troops were getting ready for class, I was getting ready to go fishing in the Snake River, Banana River, or the Atlantic Ocean. Between M.Sgt. Davis and I, we caught enough fish to feed the entire class on Thursday nights.

After two weeks at DEOMI, I called home to check on Velma and Chris. She told me the letter from WSU had arrived. She was told to open it and read it to me. She read, "Dear Mr. Wimes, congratulation—"

I interrupted her by saying, "You can stop reading. I don't need to hear anymore." The news went out all over the school that M.Sgt. James Wimes was among the elite students with a graduate degree.

DEOMI was a very intense school. Each day, I was attacked for the slightest verbal stereotype or disparaging remark. For instance, "Holy Cow" was an affront to people from India because they worship cows. The "Commander, he" is an affront to females because the commander could be a woman. Almost anything out of your mouth could be a cause for an attack by the rest of the class.

After a month, I was ready to disenroll myself, but my group advisor would not allow me. I don't remember his name, but he was the spitting image of a black Sigmund Freud with concord pipe and all. He explained to me the reason the group always attacked me. According to him, I was well educated, one of eight that qualified for the Ops Program, and just plain big and loud. As a group, there is a chance of defeating you, but as an individual, you destroy each of them with your strong personality and intellect.

DEOMI was a highly academic military school. There was a phase test each week. If you failed a test, you were given a makeup test on Monday and a weekly phase test on Friday of the same week. My best friend, T.Sgt. Dianne Dalston, failed a test and wanted to disenroll herself. I talked her into staying by promising to spend the entire weekend studying with her. We studied on Friday, Saturday, and Sunday on the beach. On Monday, T.Sgt. Dalston passed the test with flying colors. She became my constant companion and confidante. Dianne went on to become the first black female chief master sergeant and senior enlisted advisor in the Georgia Air National Guard.

A few weeks before graduation from DEOMI, I received orders for Minot AFB, North Dakota. I told my mentor before I go to "Why Not Minot"; I will fail the rest of my phase tests. In the end, I was sent back to McConnell AFB to fill my own slot.

I had one of the best trainers in the Social Actions career field. TSgt. Lacornia Harris was a family man with a very strong religious background. He taught me everything about teaching Human Relations Education (HRE) and Equal Opportunity and Treatment (EOT) counseling. Lacornia and I were a perfect pair for good cop and bad cop.

Shortly after, I got settled into my job; there was a change of command in our office. Lt. Col. Kenneth Morrison took over the chief slot from Lt. Col. Ortiz. During his first staff meeting, Col. Morrison briefed the crew that he had come to Wichita to retire. He went on to say that if he could fulfill anything on our wish list, speak up now. The troops began to hum their wish list. I did not say anything. The colonel looked at me and asked what did I want him to do for me. I said, "Colonel, I want to take my family to Clark AB, Philippines, the birthplace of Christopher.

Colonel Morrison smiled and said to me, "Your request is a piece of cake. The colonel was returning from Headquarters PACAF (Pacific Air Force) at Hickham AFB, Hawaii. He gave me information that the personnel center at Randolph AFB knew about. He told me to go to CBPO (Central Base Personnel Office) and volunteer for the M.Sgt. EOT slot at Clark AB, Philippines. CBPO told me there was not an open EOT slots at Clark AB. After several no-no's and several yes, yes, yes's, I requested to see CM.Sgt. Robert Allen. He called Hdqt. Personnel at Randolph AFB, Texas. The information was so new it had not been put into the system. I was qualified and the first to apply, so I was given the assignment. I could not wait to tell Velma and Chris about the assignment to his birthplace.

There were three major EOT incidents during my tenure at McConnell AFB. The first was when a young black airman reported to the office to file a complaint of racial slurs by a young white airman. He said they were washing a KC 135 plane when he asked the white guy to pass him the mop. The white airman said, "I don't take orders from no nigger."

I asked him, "What did you do then?"

He said, "I chased him all over the flight line but couldn't catch him. I called the unit commander and requested the young airman be sent to EOT office for an interview. The use of racial slurs is a serious offense in the military. However, one has to find humor in any job. As I began to interview the white airman and told him that he had been accused of having used racial slurs to his coworker. The white airman knew he had screwed up, so he was nervous and responded with, "What! I didn't call that nigger a nigger." The airman lost one of his two stripes because of SHIT.

The second incident involved a master sergeant, staff sergeant, and his wife at the NCO Club. The staff sergeant was there to celebrate his promotion to technical sergeant. However, his club dues were not up to date. The master sergeant being a night manager was not going to allow him into the club. Another night manager spoke up for the staff sergeant because he was with his wife. Later that evening, the black M.Sgt./night manager was walking through the club when he overheard the wife say, "Niggers think they own this damn club." The black manager went over and told the lady to watch her mouth or she would have to leave the club. The staff sergeant told the night manager that he could not talk to his wife like that and attempted to hit the night manager. However, the staff sergeant was drunk on alcohol which made him slow. The manager was sober and beat him to the punch. At that point, the wife jumped onto the manager's back at which he turned and punched her in the face.

The following Monday, the white couple reported to the base police to file assault charges and the club manager reported to the Social Actions Office to discrimination charges. The Wing Commander, Brig. Gen. Elmer Brooks had been briefed by the base police commander.

I had not finished interviewing the master sergeant when Gen. Brooks called and ordered the M.Sgt. and I to his office for a conference to resolve this situation. When we arrived at the Wing Headquarter, the white couple was already there. The general called us all into his conference room. Gen. Brooks first heard the assault complaint and then the EOT complaint. The wife admitted to making the disparaging remarks because where they were raised, they always called black people "Niggers."

Gen. Brooks passed sentence on the black night manager by giving him an administrative reduction in rank for one year and the loss of his part-time job. The general then turned to the staff sergeant and his wife for their sentence. He first addressed the young lady. She was banned from the base forever except in case of a hospital emergency. He then addressed the staff sergeant. He told him since you cannot manage your own family, it is obvious you cannot manage military troops, therefore your line number for promotion to technical sergeant has been rescinded. Oh! I forgot to mention that Brig. Elmer Brooks is an Afro American from Washington, DC. As for the master sergeant and the staff sergeant, they can testify to SHIT.

The third and final major incident involved a young airman by the name of David Adkins. He is better known now by his stage and screen name Sinbad. Airman Adkins came to my office one day to file an EOT complaint against his commander. Adkins had won a position on the Top In Blue Talent Show as a master's of ceremony with his comedy routine as Sinbad. He had participated at base, command, air force, and worldwide levels and won. For his winning, he was awarded MC of Tops in Blue and travel to bases all over the world entertaining troops for a year.

Well, as fate would have it, his CO would not permit him to go, saying he was mission essential. Sinbad, even with all his humor, was one of the tops in his field of air refueling in the USAF. The CO had allowed several other refuelers to attend a softball tournament but refused Airman Adkins. He refused to fly and was charged with "dereliction of duty." He filed an EOT complaint saying he was denied because he was black and the others were white. There was just enough evidence to cloud the water. Sinbad was given the Article 15 with a general discharge under honorable conditions at the convenience of the government but no jail time. Two years later, Sinbad returned to McConnell AFB as a superstar. In his comic routine, he credits the USAF with his success based on SHIT.

CHAPTER 14

The Family Pet

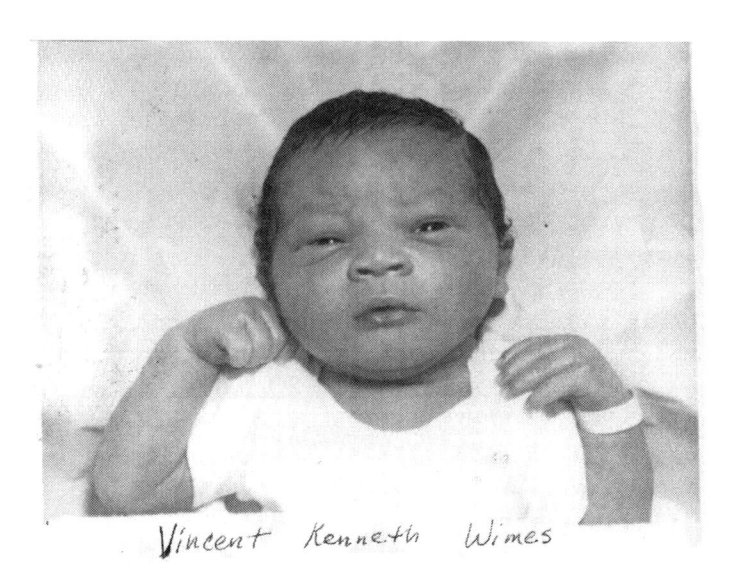

Vincent Kenneth Wimes

On March 31, 1981, Velma and I went to the NCO Club to celebrate my thirty-seventh birthday. She and I had dinner and dancing. Around 2300 hours, I suggested we go home and make a baby. Naturally, I was joking about the baby because Velma was given a tubal ligation after the miscarriage in 1980. That night, Velma gave me the biggest birthday gift ever. Of course, neither my wife nor I knew about the gift until May 1981 when her monthly period was late. Again I jokingly said to Velma, "We did make a baby on my birthday." She laughed but went to the doctor anyway. It was confirmed she was indeed pregnant. On November 24, 1981, my thirty-seventh birthday present arrived.

Velma had driven herself to the hospital for her ninth-month checkup. I was on base assisting with the office birthday party for Lt. Col. Kenneth Morrison. The office secretary came in and said, "M.Sgt. Wimes, the hospital just called and said if you want to see your child being born, you had better rush to St. Joseph Hospital as soon as possible. When I arrived at the hospital, I was asked had I attended the lamaze classes. I said no because we knew Velma would be having a cesarean section. St. Joseph Hospital believed in cradle to grave parental involvement. However, without the lamaze classes, you are not allowed in the delivery room because you may pass out during surgery. I looked at the nurse and pointed to the various Vietnam service ribbons.

"Nurse, you go tell the doctor that I am a Vietnamese vet and want to see the birth of his child." The doctor agreed that if he can handle Nam, this will be nothing, let him in.

Velma was awake during the delivery. She was given a "saddle block" which deadened her from the waist down. I talked to her during the entire operation. The doctors were so cool in their behavior. One of the doctors told Velma that her scar from Christopher's birth was ugly. He promised his scar would allow her to wear a bikini at the beach. After on hour, my thirty-seventh birthday present was born. We were hoping for a girl, but we got a healthy boy. I named him Vincent Kenneth Wimes. Kenneth was because he and Col. Kenneth Morrison shared the same birthday.

Christopher was very happy that the newest member of the family was a boy. According to Chris, he preferred a brother because girls don't know nothing. He said his friend Dax Love has a sister, and she doesn't know nothing. Christopher loves his little brother.

The Christmas and New Year holidays came and departed with the Wimes family very happy. The travel orders sending us to the Philippines were now in my hands. All we had to do was wait for August 1982. In the meantime, Velma and I continued to work. Each day, Chris went to school, and Vincent was taken to Mama Thompson house for babysitting. While waiting for my deployment date, I requested to attend Academic Instructor School (AIS) at Maxwell AFB, Alabama. The school was required for full certification as a military instructor. AIS also provided training for foreign military officer. The school afforded me the opportunity to conversate with many diverse races of people. I befriended a Malaysian army major. His English was not good, but with my help, he was successful and finished the school. Velma could not attend my graduation. However, Mama Thompson had sent her daughter Regina to Montgomery to visit some family members. She called me while she was there, so I invited her to my graduation and a free ride back to Wichita. Regina was happy because she could go shopping by cashing in her plane ticket. I was also happy because now I have someone to help me drive home.

Upon my return to Wichita, I began to out-process. I started with passport applications for Velma, Chris, Vincent, and Michael (dog). Oh yes, Michael had to have travel papers like the rest of the family. The dog did not need a passport, but he had to have travel orders and a visa.

June 1982 arrived, and school was out. In order for Velma to see her family before we left for the Philippines, I arranged for the family to fly home to Georgia. The plan was for me to drive to Georgia in two weeks to get them. When we returned to Wichita, the out-processing continued. We were allowed to ship 400 pounds of necessary house and personal effect by air.

These items would be on base the day we arrive. The household good had to be shipped by ocean vessel which can take as long as six weeks. The household goods were packed and shipped the last week of July. We stayed in Temporary Lodging for Family (TLF) for a week. On August 1, 1982, the entire family loaded up and headed west to Norton AFB, California.

The decision to drive was trifold. First was the travel pay worth 32 cent per mile from McConnell AFB, Kansas, to Norton AFB, California, times four. Secondly, I had to deliver my car to the Port of Los Angeles to be shipped to Manila. Finally, by driving to California, I could stop and visit with my friend CM.Sgt. Robert Marshall in Phoenix, Arizona. After being coped up in a car for two days with a wife, two sons, and a dog, Marshall's face was a welcoming site. We spent two days of our travel time visiting with Robert, Lorraine, and Kris. This stopover gave me a chance to rest before driving across the Mojave Desert into southern California. The visit also included taking in a movie, *An Officer and a Gentleman*, which won Louis Gossett, Jr. an Oscar for best supporting actor. The movie ended at 2200 hours and the temperature was 110 degrees. So the visit also gave me a chance to experience the heat of the desert.

We arrived at Norton AFB on Wednesday for a flight to Clark AB on Saturday. I left Kansas before we received the passport and visas for Velma and the boys. I was told these items would be waiting for me at the personnel office. Ironically, the only papers waiting for me were the papers for Michael, the dog, and me. Traffic Management Office (TMO) went into action making phone calls to Washington, DC, in an attempt to find the travel documents for Velma and the boys. The State Department said that the papers would be at Norton AFB by Thursday afternoon. At 1500 hours the documents were not on base. More calls were made to DC.

The travel papers were still at the State Department. The seriousness of the situation was explained that a service member will be forced to leave his family in California if the papers don't get to Norton AFB by Friday afternoon.

I went to the transit billeting to explain the situation to Velma. Needless to say, she could not understand that the US government was more concerned about the well-being of a dog over a family. I don't know how they accomplished this trick, but the Department of State can work miracle when they want to. In less than eighteen hours, they processed passports and visas and arranged for them to be delivered to Norton AFB, California. The next morning, the Wimes family boarded a 747 aircraft bound for Manila, Philippine Islands. With the ride from Kansas to California and the problems with the travel papers, Velma and the boys now understand that the military tries hard to eliminate situation of SHIT.

We flew directly into Manila International Airport. As we were going through customs, we were confronted with our first controversy. Michael, the dog, was the first to receive his travel papers.

However, he was the first to experience problems upon arrival in the Philippines. The custom authority told me that Michael had to be quarantined for a week at a cost of 500 pesos ($25). I quickly handed the gentleman the money. I then asked, "When may I pick up my dog?"

He smiled and said, "Oh, you can take the dog. The quarantine was the 500 pesos." We loaded our bags and belongings on a private jeepney and head for Clark AB, which was approximately sixty-five miles north of Manila.

As we entered Angeles City, Chris looked at me and asked, "Are you sure this is where I was born." He saw no sidewalks, big holes in the streets, and a thousand multicolored jeepneys with crazy driving patterns. Chris then noticed a horse-drawn chalisa, whereby the horse started to defecate in the street. Chris looked at me with a very serious look on his face. He said, "Dad, can we go back to Kansas now because I don't like where I was born." It appeared that Chris and Dorothy and Toto all wanted red shoes to click together so they could leave Oz.

We finally arrived at the main gate of Clark Air Base. Chris was impressed once we were inside the base. There is a world of difference between inside and outside the base. We moved directly into a three-bedroom house trailer with two baths, kitchen, and living room. The house trailer was our home for two months. The first order of business was to hire a house girl (maid) to babysit Vincent. To find a house girl, I needed to find my friends. I started at a place called *Friends and Strangers*. It was part café and part bar. The owner and I had been friends since 1965 during my first assignment in the Philippines. His name was Philander Rodman, better known as Pelie, which means rice in English. Many of you are more familiar with his famous son Dennis Rodman of the NBA Chicago Bulls.

I told Pelie I needed a house girl. He quickly recommended a niece of his wife. Her name was Ryder Robles. I met the young lady and hired her on the spot. Ryder had not been in Angeles City long enough to get tainted by the horny military men. In other words, she was not a garden tool, if you know what I mean. Ryder took to Vincent immediately. Vincent became her baby. In fact, she took to Vincent so well that Christopher got jealous and concerned that Ryder was going to steal his little brother. At thirty years of age, Vincent is still Ryder's baby.

Velma got a job with DODDS (Department of Defense Dependent Schools) teaching middle school special needs students. Each day, she would come home with stories about her students. Her most special student was a young boy born with his brain outside his head. He was born without a complete skull. The doctors at Clark Air Base Hospital designed a metal cap to fit over his exposed brain and anchored it to his head. Other than the metal skull, he was all boy!

Chris was enrolled in middle school. His teacher was Ms. Johnson. Ms. Johnson was a full-figured lady with super large breasts. Well, one day, she called Chris a lie in class. She was teaching current events that day and the subject was the USS Kitty Hawk Carrier hitting a Russian submarine in the South China Sea. Well, Chris told the teacher and class that he had been on that ship two weeks prior. She told Chris to stop lying because the USS Kitty Hawk was out to sea. My son was hurt because he knew he was telling the truth. Chris came home that afternoon and asked me the name of the ship we visited at Subic Bay Navy Base. I replied, "It was the USS Kitty Hawk."

Christopher responded with, "I told that big tittie woman I was on that ship."

After regaining my composure from laughing, I quickly verbally reprimanded Chris. However, I went to the school the next day to let Ms. Johnson know that she owed my son an apology, for he was neither imaging nor lying about his experience touring the USS Kitty Hawk.

This being my third assignment to Clark Air Base made me feel right at home. Of course, this was the first time being assigned to the largest Social Actions Office in the military. The EOT office was manned by a captain, lieutenant, senior master sergeant, three master sergeants, a technical sergeant, and two staff sergeants. The Drug and Alcohol Abuse Office was twice the size of EOT. The entire office was under the command of Lt. Col. Laughlin. Col. Laughlin was one of the fairest commanders that I have ever known. Our main jobs were human relations education, investigating EOT complaints, and Staff Assistance Visits (SAV), which was analyzing the human relations climate for a unit commander. I remember a SAV to a fighter unit with a population of three hundred men and thirty women. The story unfolded when a female went AWOL (absent without leave) for a week. Her commander was going to give her an Article 15 punishment which was to take one of her three stripes.

Well, she files an EOT complaint under the provision of Sexual Harassment as outlined in Air Force Regulation 30-2. In order to be sure that this was not the case in his fighter squadron, the commander called for a SAV by our office. I was chosen to head up the SAV team.

We reported to the commander to give him his in-briefing as well as find out if there are any particular points of interest he was concerned about. While waiting for the commander, I noticed that his clerk had an almost nude picture on his desk. I told him that the picture created an intimidating or hostile environment. He said that is a picture of my wife. My response was, "I don't care if it is your mother. It has no place in this administrative office." The intimidating environment didn't stop there. The entire team reported to the commander's office. The first thing I observed was on the wall behind the commander's desk was two bronze softballs with a plaque that read, "To Belong To This Unit You Got To Have Balls."

The SAV was downhill from there. We conducted a survey of the entire unit and the data revealed that the human relation climate did not include females in a positive light. The graffiti in the latrine stalls indicated unfavorable thoughts of women in fighter squadron.

To understand the fighter unit mentality, one must understand that in 1982, women were not allowed to pilot fighter aircraft. Women were trained in T-38 aircraft, which are fighter-type planes. In fact, some countries use the T-38 as their fighter warplane. Once a female completed training, they were usually assigned to Military Airlift Command (MAC) to fly cargo aircraft, such as the C-135, C-141, and the C-5.

The SAV team spent a week in the fighter unit gathering compelling data to support a claim of sexual harassment based on an "intimidating and hostile environment." When we conducted the out-briefing, the commander seemed surprised or insensitive to our findings. He just did not want to accept that his unit was in sensitive to issues involving females.

Finally, I pointed to the plaque behind his desk. I said to him, "Sir, based on your office, no female will ever belong to this unit because God did not bless them with balls. If there are no further questions, this SAV is complete." The team came to the position of attention, saluted, and departed.

Now back to the sergeant that went AWOL. The administrative punishment was dropped. She used the system to get away, but she was guilty as sin. The SAV revealed that she went AWOL to spend time with her boyfriend before he returned to the good old USA. As for the commander, he was reassigned with the full impact of SHIT.

My third tour at Clark AB was going beautiful until there was a change of command at every level of the base. However, it was the change of command in the Social Actions Office had a direct impact on me. The old captain was replaced by Capt. Brown, Col. Laughlin was replaced by Maj. Dennett, and SM.Sgt. Don Hughes was replaced by SM.Sgt. Ralph Brown. SM.Sgt. Brown ate like a horse and never gained an ounce. He had this thing against anyone that was not skinny. He stayed on me and M.Sgt. Stan Johnson; we were both healthy in size.

However, SM.Sgt. Brown paid for his mistreatment of Stan and me. As soon as he sewed on his E-8 stripes, he started acting like a pure fool. He finally tore his behind when signed Maj. Dennett name to an endorsement letter and sent it to the Commander of Thirteenth Air Force (Lt. General). The letter had a misspelled word and was sent back for corrections. At that point, SM.Sgt. Brown decided not to make the corrections because he knew the major had not authorized a general's endorsement for him. When the stuff hit the fan, he was given an Article 15 in lieu of a court martial. He was reduced in rank by one stripe which made his date of rank three years less than mine. If he had stayed in Social Actions, I would have been his supervisor. The air force felt that it would not have been a good idea to have someone tainted working in such a prestigious position as Superintendent of Social Actions. Not to mention working for someone, he tried to screw over for being heavy, not overweight, just heavy. M.Sgt. Brown finished his career passing out basketball and towels in the base gym.

I became the NCOIC of Social Action but that when my troubles began to escalate. I do believe that Maj. Dennette told his replacement (Maj. Boler) that he had gotten M.Sgt. Brown, and it was up to him to get the other M.Sgt. (me). From the first day he arrived, I was his target. Maj. Boler looked at everything I was involved in with a microscope. What is worst was he directed the newly assigned Capt. Brown to do his dirty work. The two of them almost drove me crazy. I actually had to go see the psychiatrist if I were crazy. I did everything I could do to impress those two fools, one black and one white, to no avail.

I participated in a commercial for the youth center. When the commercial aired, my two supervisors said I looked fat even those I was under my maximum weight. I had the Air Force Television Network (AFTN) to write a letter that said TV cameras always make the subject appear 10 to 15 pounds heavier. The major directed me to be placed on the weight management program under AFReg.39-11.

I was directed to write an article for the Philippine Flyer Base Newspaper. I wrote the article, and it was published. The title was "Sexual harassment is not only a female problem." My article was the only published article from any person in the entire office. However, when I got my airmen performance report (APR), it stated my writing ability was nonexistent. This particular APR will be discussed later when I tell about my return from my last assignment to my beloved P.I. Maj. Boler and Capt. Brown cauterized me in the same boat with newly demoted M.Sgt. Brown. I think sometimes they were jealous of the fact that I was an enlisted person with five college degrees, and they were officers with only two at best.

As a human relations education instructor for the NCO Preparatory Academy, the graduates chose me to be their graduation speaker. I was thrilled to be chosen for such an honor. However, when I was introduced as the speaker and my alcaldes and college degrees were given, the deputy base commander responded out loud, "Damn, when did he have time to be just a Master Sergeant."

Oftentimes I am asked, "Why do you love the Philippines so much?" Well, besides the warm weather, there were the warm ladies. The P.I. is the only place in the world where it is almost impossible to find an ugly woman. The cost of living is so cheap that an E-7 could live like a king.

I made more money legally than a Filipino senator. No matter how ugly an airman may have been, there is a living doll he could have for his bed fellow. In fact, if you had anything going for you, there were dozens of beautiful ladies at your beck and call. My attributes were above average, so I had it made. First of all, I spoke Tagolog (National language of the Philippines) almost fluently after three tours which added to me being sought after. I still speak Tagolog to Filipinos every chance I get. I also wore my uniform in direct compliance with Air Force Reg. 35-10; nothing was ever out of place. In other words, I looked good in my clothes. Finally, I was an athlete. I played on the base tennis team and played on one of the six American football teams. I officiated every sport but basketball. On game nights, all the young ladies would be just waiting for an invitation to go on base to see any American sport. Oh, having a car was always a plus.

Earlier, I wrote about Philander Rodman, father of the famous Dennis Rodman. Pelie, as we called him, was the owner of two nightclubs and restaurant: Friends & Strangers and Friends & Strangers Too. There were several beautiful women working as waitresses and hostesses. However, when I finally took time to visit the area to relax and have fun, I noticed a very light-skinned young lady. She was introduced to me as Barbara Evarlie, Pelie's sister-in-law. Barbara and I remain friends to this day. She and her daughter Jamaca lives in St. Louis, Missouri.

As a member of the NCO Club, one would go there each workday for lunch and dessert of eye candy (beautiful young ladies dancing in (bikinis). One day, I went to lunch mainly for the dessert and was thrilled when what was to me the prettiest Filipino lady I had ever seen. She had long black hair that reached the calves of her gorgeous legs. Yes, I was a married man with two fine sons. However, I am a man with good eyes and especially for eye candy.

After all, just because a man is fat, it does not mean he can't read the menu. This young lady danced with the grace and moves of an angel. Well, I sent her a note that said, "Please call me tomorrow with the base extension number." The next day, I received a call from a lady by the name of Elizabeth Senita.

We talked for a long time and shared information about one another. Beth, as she preferred to be called, told me she was sent notes every day that she dances, but I was the only man that said, "Please call me" instead of just an extension on base. Beth and I became the best of friends. She had a steady (live-in boyfriend), and I had a wife. She had two daughters, and I had two sons. We had to live on the edge to maintain a healthy life at home with our families. Beth became my very close friend and traveling companion. As a member of the base tennis team, I traveled all over the Philippines.

On my birthday, March 31, 1984, we played a tournament in Bagio City of northern Luzon Island. I was told by our coach that I needed to be on my best behavior because the president's sister would be playing with the Manila Tennis team. I assumed he was talking about the president of the Manila Tennis Club. It was not until a mixed doubles match was slated between this little old lady and her male partner and my female partner and me. Coach Lucky came to me again to remind me to watch my mouth. It was at that time the chair empire excused himself and was replaced by a man with a large canvas bag. That gentleman was the bodyguard for Baby Marcus Barber, the baby sister of President Ferdinand Marcus. The canvas bag contained a Thompson Sub Machine Gun. Needless to say, the match was over before it started. Mrs. Barber team won 6-2, 6-1. I think the machine gun was their best serve and volley.

After the match, it was announced that it was my fortieth birthday. Mrs. Barber sent a note to the Camp John Hay NCO Club and ordered a birthday party for James Wimes and forty of his guest for his fortieth birthday. I even had a four-star general from the Filipino Air Force write me a poem that was read during the party as they served the ice cream and cake.

The Wimes family continued to live the high life in the P.I. The base provided all the activities needed for a family. Chris participated in football, basketball and soccer. He was scared to play baseball from fear of the ball hitting him. He would go to the baseball games when I officiated. Velma spent her time at the hobby shop and square dancing. Each year the Silver Wings Service Club sponsored a "Real Men Cooks" event. I entered two recipes for Wimes' Bake Beans and Wimes' Land Sea and Air Salad. I won second place for the salad and third place for the beans.

Time passes fast when you are having fun. August 1985 was fast approaching with time for us to say good-bye to the Philippines. I had received the perfect assignment. The USAF had reassigned me to Tornado Alley or McConnell

AFB, Kansas. We were all happy, especially Chris and Velma. Chris was happy because of his best friend, Dax Love, Velma because of her ability to get a job in education. We were all happy because we were going home to our little house on South Santa Fe.

I went to see Beth to tell her I had received my assignment to return to Kansas. She was both happy and sad. She was happy because she knew I had gotten the assignment I was hoping for. Beth was sad because she was about to lose one of her closest friends. Around the middle of July 1985, I went to visit Beth again, and she asked if she could have $50 to finish paying for my going-away present. Well, I gave her the money. We saw a lot of one another as July passed, and finally it was August. Three days before we were to depart, I went to see Beth, and she started crying. She apologized for not having my going-away gift. She said that the gift would not be ready before I was to leave the Philippines. My first thought was Beth had conned me out for fifty bucks and didn't know what to say in her good-byes.

I went to bid all my friends farewell and good-bye, for I was off to Wichita, Kansas. All they could say to me and the family was SHIT.

CHAPTER 15

Back to the Land of Oz Once More

We were very happy to be returning to McConnell AFB, Kansas, but moreover, I was happy to be returning to the family house. While we were in the Philippines, the house was under lease. The family that my property manager had leased the house to this day owes me about $2,000. The nonpaying family tore up my house. To give you an example of what I mean is they used a closet door as the backboard for dart game. Needless to say, I was pissed off. That fat head, 300 lbs. of nothing had the nerve to be upset when he was told he had two weeks to vacate my house.

When I reported to the Social Actions office to meet my new supervisor, I was given more SHIT than I could handle. Maj. Boler had called Lt. Stahl and told her he was sending her the worst master sergeant in the Social Actions career field. Lt. Stahl would walk into the EOT office and bypass me (E-7) to discuss office business with S.Sgt. Pete Peterson whom I trained before going to the Philippines for the third time.

After several incidents of this nature, I finally had my fill and demanded a conference with Lt. Stahl. She was told quite simply that the USAF has a principle that establishes rank, order, and precedence. I had the rank. I had the order, and she needed to understand the precedence. If these regulations could not be adhered to, she and I needed to see the wing commander for my transfer. She then informed me that she was warned by Maj. Boler that I was a bad seed and would eat a young female lieutenant alive. I assured her that if given the chance, I would make her look good. At that point, she began to put a little trust in me. S.Sgt. Peterson, whom she did trust, validated my knowledge of all of Social Actions to her also helped. The action by Maj. Boler also awakened me to the inevitable. I knew he was going to see that I would receive a very bad Airman Performance Report (APR).

I made friends quickly being one of the first persons newly assigned personnel meet during their in-processing. Also my old friend from Germany, CM.Sgt. Allen, was still NCOIC of the personnel office. I let him, and one of his subordinates, know that I was expecting a bad APR, and I *want* to know the minute it hit the base. Well, it finally arrived, and one of my new friends called and said, "Sgt. Wimes, you need to see this APR, it is the worst I have ever seen on a master sergeant." I rushed to personnel to see this big lie that had been bestowed upon me.

The contents of that APR was so bad that all I could do was cry. Much worst, the major had a black captain to write this APR with full knowledge it was a lie. Maj. Boler was trying to fulfill Maj. Dennett's wishes. The APR denied me reenlistment with an overall rating of six out of nine.

A master sergeant would get a seven by being alive in a dirty uniform. The young airman said she would not process the APR until I had a chance to reenlist because I had more than twenty years of service I could reup (reenlist) whenever I wanted to. Within one week, I had reenlisted with the newest 2nd Lt. on base to give me the oath of enlistment. With my career back intact, my next task was to prove my last APR was bogus and a big lie put together by Capt. Brown and Maj. Boler.

I hated those two sorry excuses for officers so much that I awakened Velma one night and told her I was going to take out a contract on their lives. It was the thought of more than twenty years of doing the right thing and having it ruined on one sheet of paper. Velma and I talked until dawn. She convinced me that what I was thinking was wrong and sinful. We decided that I should return to the Philippines to gather evidence to refute that APR and have it thrown out of my records.

The first thing I did was to get me a civilian passport and visa granted by the Philippine government. I also bought a round trip airline ticket. I went to the PI strictly as an American civilian. This way, when I went on base to confront Maj. Boler, I would be under the protection of Manila, not the military. During the two weeks I was there, visits were made to several commanders and requested letters attesting to my positive character and professionalism.

I went to see Maj. Boler. He was then the commander of headquarters squadron. I had only one question for that sorry excuse of a man, "What did I do to deserve the APR that he had dictated?" The major had no reason. He was also told that he had done enough damage to my career, and it was time to stop. I returned home to start paperwork on having the APR thrown out of my personnel files.

For guidance, I called my formal Chief of Social Actions at Clark Air Base, Lt. Col. Laughlin. I explained to him my intentions and what I had done so far. He quickly told me that I needed more than letters from commanders. Col. Laughlin said he would have to think of some strategies. A month later, he got back to me with a foolproof way of having the APR removed. During our conversation, it was mentioned that Capt. Brown was on Temporary Duty (TDY) the majority of the reporting period. The reporting period was the key we needed. Air force regulation states: "in order for a supervisor to be authorized write an APR on a subordinate, one must 120 days of consecutive supervision."

When I returned to the personnel office with this information, I was reprimand for not revealing the days of supervision from the start. The APR section of personnel obtained the TDY orders of Capt. Brown for the reporting period of the APR. The longest consecutive period of supervision was eighty-three days. The package was sent to USAF Headquarters for an analysis. Within four weeks, I received a letter and a copy of the Letter Of Evaluation (LOE) that would replace the bogus APR. The LOE was signed by a four-star general. I was happy but still angry because nothing was done to those dirty rats for trying to ruin my career.

With my career back on track, I could now concentrate on helping Lt. Stahl run a ship shape social actions office. After being put on the weight program in the Philippines, there was never a peaceful moment. Each day, I went to the gym to sweat off a pound or two because I never knew when the orderly room would call me in to be weighted.

Well, one day while I was melting away pounds in the sauna, a conversation started about IG (Inspector General) hitting McConnell AFB. I knew that the IG rumor was based on facts because the sauna was standing room only with fat men sweating off weight. I immediately hurried back to the office to brief Lt. Stahl. She was her normal self, know it all. I was told that her girlfriend does the travel orders for the IG, and if they were coming to our base, her friend would give her a "heads up." Lt. Stahl was asked if it would be okay for me to conduct a self-inspection of the EOT section. She agreed to me doing the self-inspection of the Human Relation and Equal Opportunity Sections. I went over those sections with a fine-tooth comb. The purpose of a self-inspection is to find problem areas and start making corrections before the IG inspectors. The IG cannot use self-inspection items in their evaluations.

Two weeks passed with the daily sauna room and track filled to capacity with GIs trying to sweat off a few pounds before the IG arrives. In order for me to lose about ten pounds, I took high blood pressure pills to urinate and milk of magnesium to have bowel movements twice a day. Yes, I know drugs can kill you, but without my air force career, my family would suffer.

Well, another week was about to pass and no IG. Then as the Baptist preacher say, "Early, early on Thursday morning, a C-135 aircraft hit the runway and off stepped the SAC Inspector General. The phone tree was set into action with all personnel reporting to the base. By the time I arrived at work, the Social Actions Office had received its first negative report against the Chief of Social Action, Lt. Sue Stahl. The inspector had a problem finding the office. According to Air Force Regulation 30-2 the office of Social Actions must be centrally located and easily identified. Lt. Stahl was about to have a SHIT.

It was at that point, I the worst master sergeant in the air force, became very important to her existence. "M.Sgt. Wimes, what am I going to do?" That tall senior master sergeant (SM.Sgt.) is going to give me an unsatisfactory evaluation. I didn't say to her "I told you so," but she knew what I was thinking. No matter who the chief may have been, if the office failed, we all failed. That would mean that Maj. Boler would have been right about me.

The IG inspector convened a meeting of the entire staff for an in-briefing. It was at that time I noticed a "square and compass" ring on the left hand of the SM.Sgt. Headquarter SAC had sent me a savior. Headquarters SAC had sent me a traveling man. I gave him the sign, and from then on, I knew failure was not an option. The inspector's first inspection was of the facility. Around noon, the inspector asked for a place to get lunch. Being the big brother with a 32nd Degree ring, it was only fitting that I take the inspector to lunch. He and I went to Aloha Chinese Restaurant for the best buffet in Wichita, Kansas. We talked for the better part of two hours. During that conversation, I knew the office was not getting an unsatisfactory rating. Of course, Lt. Stahl was worrying all to hell. I could not tell her that she had "nothing to fear but fear itself." However, I kept encouraging her. That Friday evening, the SM.Sgt. asked her if he could have a few drug and alcohol case files to take to his hotel room to review during the weekend. "You guessed it." My supervisor told the IG, "No, he could not."

My Masonic brother came to me and asked, "Is she a fool or what?" She told him to take the files from the office and to be on a "need to know" bases. All I could do was assure him that by the end of the day, he would have as many files as wanted.

I went to my boss's office and closed the door. I asked her, "Are you out of your damn mind"? That man represents Headquarter SAC Social Actions, and he has the authority and need to know anything in any drug and alcohol file in this damn office. You can rest assure that if he doesn't get those files, this whole drug and alcohol program will bite the dust. Give him what he wants, and you will not get an unsatisfactory rating.

That Monday morning was the out-briefing to the wing commander. Lt. Stahl attended the briefing and was given a copy of the details. The rating for the EOT/HRE Section of Social Actions was outstanding. The rating for Drug and Alcohol Section was marginal. The overall rating of the Social Actions Office was satisfactory, and with the guidance of M.Sgt. James E. Wimes an outstanding rating was forthcoming. Lt. Stahl was flabbergasted that I was mentioned by name during the out-briefing. It appears that the worst master sergeant in the USAF had been elevated to the top of the Social Actions career field.

Lt. Stahl and I actually became friends. She began to confide in me on a personal level. Of course, S.Sgt. Peterson remained her number one staff member, but I had gained the respect that a twenty-plus-year master sergeant is supposed to have. The joke was that I was in the USAF before my supervisor was born. In fact, the base commander called one day and said to me, "Get your daughter (Lt. Stahl) and both of you report to my office." To add to her problem of fraternization, she wanted to have her wedding at the McConnell AFB Chapel. All hell broke loose between the base chaplain and the base commander. The base commander said that he would not allow an officer to marry an enlist airman on McConnell AFB. The base chaplain went over his head to Headquarters SAC with the argument that, "I don't marry officers and enlistees, I marry people in love." Lt. Stahl was married in the base chapel and very soon after shipped out to Europe.

She was to be replaced by Capt. Palmer as the new chief of social actions. However, the day he was to report to Social Actions, he was reassigned to the Base Headquarters Squadron as the unit commander. SAC was notified that McConnell AFB Social Action Office was without a chief. CM.Sgt. Grady

Parks was the superintendent of Social Actions for all SAC bases. He was told to find a replacement for McConnell AFB. His response was, M.Sgt. James E. Wimes has been running that office for the last year, so name him the new chief until a replacement can be found. The worst master sergeant in career field became the first enlisted Chief of Social Actions on a major USAF base. For the next six months, I served as the chief. I undoubtedly did a good job. My staff on both sides of the office stayed on task, and not one commander complained about the service we provided. The pressure of being an enlisted airman serving as chief in a high-profile position certainly has it effects of SHIT.

Chapter 16

My Miracle Child

Kunsan Air Base, South Korea, needed an EOT NCOIC. The year was 1987 and had completed more than twenty-four years of military service. When the assignment was offered to me, I had a choice to accept it or retire. To get maximum pay, I needed twenty-six years of service. Negotiations were now in order. I wanted the assignment, but I also wanted to return to Dorothy and Toto Country. The people at the personnel office promised me a follow-on assignment to McConnell AFB, Kansas, and my family. I was happy to be going to the "Coon" as it is affectionately called by all personnel that were ever assigned to the 8th Tactical Fighter Wing, Kunsan AB, South Korea. This unit was made famous during the Vietnam War by Brig. Gen. Robin Olds and Col. Daniel "Chappie" James. Col. James later became the first four stars general in the USAF and commander of NORAD. This assignment to the "Coon" was also ironic because I was replacing my friend M.Sgt. Cornelous George Glover whom replaced me at Clark AB, Philippines, and had orders to replace me at McConnell AFB, Kansas. M.Sgt. Glover later replaced me again after we had retired at a drug counseling center (NEDARTS) in Wichita when I resigned to become a high school.

One afternoon, a call came to the office for the NCOIC of EOT/HRE. The call was transferred to that office and answered by a female T.Sgt. It was at that time Capt. Roselyn Brown said I need to speak to M.Sgt. James E. Wimes. The T.Sgt. corrected the caller by saying, "You mean M.Sgt. James Wimes, the Chief of Social Actions? One moment, please." Capt. Brown and I talked for almost an hour. She was concerned about me coming to Kunsan AB as her superintendent. That snake Maj. Boler had briefed her about the negativity I had encountered under his supervision. When the conversation ended, I thought everything was straightened out, but apparently she still had some concerns.

Capt. Brown was informed that I would be taken a delay en route (stopover) for a week at Clark Air Base. The delay was during the same time as the Pacific Air Force (PACAF) was conducting a social actions training conference. My new chief was asked if I may attend the training since I was going to be there anyway. She reluctantly agreed. Little did I know she had sent a female staff sergeant to the conference to gather information for her about myself. What the staff sergeant didn't know was that civilian, Mr. Joe Ford, and I were personal friends and had been for more than twenty years. Joe Ford informed me that Capt. Brown had sent spies to check on me. He told the young lady that the only problem I had was the love of women, telling the truth and speaking his mind.

A week later, I arrived at Kunsan Air Base. Capt. Brown's first remark to me was, "May I see you in my office?" She began to lay down "what was expected of me." After an hour of her SHIT, I became a twenty-four-year master sergeant. She was told that I do not appreciate being chewed out by anybody before being asked, "How is your family? How was your flight? Are you hungry? Etc., etc." She was then told if she did not want me at Kunsan AB, we should discuss it with the wing commander. Who knows, he just may send me back to my family in Kansas. "Whatever the case, I don't have to accept this type of treatment from anybody and especially a junior captain." It was at that point Capt. Brown realized what her spy had briefed her about me was true. She apologized and a beautiful friendship developed.

The rest of my in-processing went extremely well until I asked to be excused from the education briefing. The education counselor said, "No, you need to hear this because of your future." She was told they had nothing to offer me in higher education. She said, "Do you have your associate degree?"

I said, "I have two associates."

"Then you should start on your bachelor's degree."

I said, "I have two bachelor's."

She said, "I suppose you are going to tell me you have two master's."

I said, "No, I don't have two masters, but I do have one master's degree and have begun working on my doctorate in education supervision."

She said, "Okay, you can be excused but report to the education service officer. We can always use more teachers at Central Texas College." I became a college instructor, teaching sociology to military personnel. While at Central Texas College, I was asked to substitute in a typing class. The regular instructor was fired after I reported to the educational officer he had not taught the students the keyboard after six weeks of a twelve-week course. The entire class was given permission to take the class again for free.

My supervisor was enrolled in the graduate school. When it was reported that I was teaching college courses, Capt. Brown recruited me to assist in writing many of her college papers and reports. I was elated that she now trusted my intellect enough; I could help her in grad school.

As a master sergeant, I was given extra funds to live off base. I found a great two-bedroom apartment in Kunsan City. Once my 1985 Chrysler Cardoba arrived, I was living in fat city. I was living in an apartment of base and a car to travel all over South Korea, especially Seoul, Korea.

One day, a staff member said she wanted me to meet a friend of hers. She told me his name was M.Sgt. Pete Blaylock, and he was NCOIC of the command center. I thought to myself, *can this be Peter Blaylock?* However, as NCOIC of the command center, one must be able to talk well and fast. My Peter Blaylock stuttered so bad it would take him ten minutes to speak to my sister. One afternoon, my traveling partner, M.Sgt. Peter Blaylock of Atlanta, Georgia, walked into my office.

He greeted me with a big hug and a Masonic sign of brotherhood. We talked about old times for the rest of our tour at the "Coon." He had gone to a speech therapist and defeated his stuttering problem. I was proud of my homeboy because we had come a long ways from selling blood.

Kunsan Air Base became a great assignment. Capt. Brown was a great supervisor. She also believed in professional development. She would send her staff to staff development conferences no matter where the location. Once she sent the entire EOT/HRE staff from the Coon to California to attend the Tuskegee Airmen Conference. We were allowed to take a "Hop" (military flight) ten days before the convention. With the ten days wait time, I went to visit my family in Kansas. The Tuskegee Airmen Convention was more than

I could have ever imagined; there were so many great black military giants there, such as Gen. Fig Newton, Lt. General Marcie Jordan, Brig. Gen. Elmer Brooks. (USAF), Lt. Gen. Frank Peterson (USM), Adm. Samuel Gravely (USN), and Gen. Roscoe Robinson, Jr. (USA) just to name a few.

Once we returned to Kunsan AB, it was business as usual. Korea is known for cold weather. In the spring and summer, the weather is quite warm. When I was not at work, my time was spent on the tennis courts. There was this young black lieutenant that challenged me to a tennis match. Yes, I beat him 6-2 and 6-2. Boy, was he upset to have been beating by a forty-four-year-old man! He was so upset that he issued another challenge with a wager. The wager was his Head Author Ashe Composite Racket to my Wilson Aluminum Oversize Racket. The word went out to the base personnel that the Legal Office and the Social Actions Office were having another tennis match. The young man verses the old man to regain his self-respect. The match became newsworthy, and a large number of people reported to the courts to see that young lieutenant take advantage of that old master sergeant. Lt. Jones was defeated 6-2, 6-2 and lost his beloved racket Excalibur. He and I played almost daily, and he never won a match because wisdom prevails over youth.

My family was the benefactor of my tour in Korea. The shopping in Seoul (E-Tae-won), Korea, would drive the average American woman crazy. I sent my sons new jogging suits every payday with their names engraved over their hearts. They had every color but pink. They were also sent matching Nike shoes for every jogging suit.

As for Velma's gifts from Korea, she was sent a 100 percent brass queen-size bed with several mink blankets. The entire family received their own personal set of luggage with their names stitched on the sides. Velma received at least two of every designer handbag and purses known at that time. What made the shopping as good as it was because of the prices being next to nothing.

The final story about my job at the Coon was going on staff assistance visit to other bases such as Taegu, Kwongju, and Pusan Air Bases. As a testament to my human relations education instructions, I was again requested to give the graduation address at the NCO Preparatory School. On my second day of a SAV to Pusan AB, I received a call from Capt. Brown. She said the base commander had requested on behalf of the graduates that I speak at their graduation. The students had heard me speak during HRE classes and wanted a dynamic senior NCO to give the closing address, M.Sgt. James E. Wimes. I said, "Capt. Brown, tell him I am TDY."

She responded, "I can't tell the base commander no."

So I had to call the base commander and explain that the wing commander had directed our office to conduct the SAV at Pusan AB. I did promise him he had a speaker for the next NCO Preparatory School graduation.

S.H.I.T—Servicemen Have It Tough

I received my orders and was disappointed. I had been promised a follow-on assignment to McConnell AFB, Kansas. However, my orders were to Moody AFB, Georgia. All my military life, my assignment wish list included Robins, Dobbins, and Moody Air Force Bases. The one time, I requested McConnell and other bases in the Midwest I get sent to Georgia. The Ironic thing about the whole ordeal is the man I replaced in Korea, that replaced me in the Philippines, was now sent to replace me in Kansas. Is that not the epitome of SHIT?

I called Velma and told her that we were going to Moody AFB, Georgia. This assignment was good and bad. It was good because Georgia was where both families lived. It was bad I would have to uproot the family from our home in Kansas. Velma would force to leave her teaching position. Vincent would have to leave his friends. Velma was not happy at all.

Like any good airman, M.Sgt. Wimes accepted his fate with open arms. After all, I only had to be in Georgia for ten months before I retired on September 1, 1988. My twenty-six-year goal would be complete on August 22, 1988. Needless to say, I was not a happy camper. The USAF had lied to me about a follow-on assignment to Kansas. The USAF had served me large dish of SHIT.

When I arrived in Wichita, Kansas, the family and friends were elated to have me home. I was granted a thirty-day leave/vacation and eight days travel time to Moody AFB, Georgia. However, Velma was not moving, and school was about to start, so I cut my vacation short. We traveled to Georgia in a brand-new burgundy 1989 Chrysler LeBron that had been delivered in Wichita. We stopped in Macon and Reynolds, Georgia, before reporting to Moody AFB in Valdosta, Georgia. We were given TLF (Temporary Lodging for Family). Velma and the boys stayed with me for one week before flying home to Wichita, Kansas.

During in-processing, I met another NCO, T.Sgt. Benny Harden. We agreed to find a house and share the expenses. I found a beautiful pad that we both could call home. Between the two of us, the house was filled with fine furniture. He was single, and I was married, but after a couple of months, I began to think I too was single. I met several young ladies but none spurred my interest. By December 1988, the Christmas parties were in full swing. One night Benny asked me to go to a party with him. The party was boring as Sunday school on Halloween. When we were about to leave, in walked this little bow, hairy-legged fox. She introduced herself as Sandra Straughter. At that point, I was ready to play more Bid Whiz (card game).

Sandra was given my number and asked if we could do lunch sometime. Well, a couple of days later, she called and asked if she and her cousin Faye could stop by the house. Being the great cook I am, I asked, "What would you like for dinner?"

She responded with, "You can surprise me."

I laid out bacon fried cabbage, home-fried onion potatoes, and pork chops. For dessert, I baked a lemon pound cake and topped it with sweet Georgia peaches. All this food was to be washed down with sweet tea or beer.

Sandra was hooked and so was Faye. Sandra was hooked on me and my cooking. Faye was just hooked on my cooking. Sandra became my constant house guest. She also became my biggest problem. We spent every spare moment together, and when we were not together, we were on the phone making plans to be together. Even when I went to visit Velma and the boys, Sandra and I found a way to communicate. Velma became suspicious and began to look for things, and when a person looks for stuff, he or she usually find a lot of SHIT.

Adrian, Sandra's only child, hated me because he felt I was taking his mother from him. I tried everything within reason to get along with that boy, with nothing working. To add fuel to the fire, Sandra's mother was against the relationship as much as her grandson. Her mother Irene felt I was too old for mid-twenties daughter. However, Sandra was hooked. She was hooked on travel, food, gifts, and loving. I issued them all too well.

I took Sandra on trips from Florida to Washington, DC, from Georgia to Kansas and all points in between. On a trip to Washington, DC, to attend the Tuskegee Airmen's Conference, she and Adrian were introduced to several black US military generals to include Gen. Elmer Brooks, Gen. Fig Newton, and Adm. Gravely. Adrian was not impressed. However, he did thank me many years later.

Cooking is something that I just love to do. In contrast to my cooking, Sandra loved to eat. She would call and ask me, "What's for dinner?" She worked at J C Penny Store, and I would cook a meal and deliver it to the job for her hot lunch.

As for the gifts, Sandra was given a diamond ring, watches, and once a car, which she did not accept. She and I went on many dates some of which were formal affairs. We once attended the Ebony Fashion Fair. That night she wore a black-and-white after-five dress and I was decked out in a tailor-made black tux. As a couple, we looked great. Working at J C Penny provided her with all the necessities she needed at home, especially when she stepped out. The one gift Sandra always enjoyed was flowers. I would send roses to her job just to hear the joy in her voice when she would call to thank me.

Prior to leaving Kusan AB, I fell on some ice and developed a tingling sensation in my ring and pinky fingers on my right hand. The PA (physician assistant) at Moody AFB Hospital wrote an order for me to see the specialist at Keesler AFB Medical Center in Biloxie, Mississippi.

When I arrived at Keesler Medical Center, I was given a thorough examination. Regular X-ray didn't show anything abnormal. However, when the doctor did a nerve conduction study, there was just enough problem to warrant further exams. I was sent to New Orleans, Louisiana, for a new type of X-ray known as MRI (magnetic resonance imaging). This type of X-ray shows a cross section of the spinal cord and spinal column. When the X-rays were read at Keesler Medical Center on Thursday, the doctors called me in with some startling results. It was determined that I had severe compression of my spinal cord at the C3—C7 section of my neck. The neurosurgeon said the only other time he had seen a case that bad was on a quadriplegic. The doctors wanted to operate the next day. I told them, "No way were you cutting me the next day. I had been complaining for more than eighteen months about the pain in my neck and the tingling in my fingers. I was going home to Georgia and would be back next week for the operation." Needless to say, the doctors were not pleased. The doctors told me that the slightest jolt to my neck could render me paralyzed from the neck down. As I departed Keesler AFB for home, a big storm occurred that made me think about the doctor's comments every step of the way.

The next week, I had Sandra drive me to Keesler for the operation. While I was in the hospital, she was allowed to keep my car. The thought of having an operation on my spinal cord scared me senseless. The surgery consisted of cutting through the front of my throat and removing three vertebrate and replacing them with bones from the bone bank. The operation went well. The new bones processed a canal large enough for my spinal cord to expand to a normal diameter which is roughly the size of a quarter. I stayed in the hospital for two weeks after which Sandra returned to Keesler too because to drive me to Valdosta. I was given a thirty-day convalescent leave. After three days at home, my hormones became active. Sandra and I hooked up, and to my surprise, my penis stood erect as a flag pole in the center of Moody, but I did not feel anything.

When I told Sandra, her response was to touch the penis-wenie. I had no feeling at all in my penis. She was told to pinch my little soldier as hard as she could. She almost pinched the skin off my soldier standing at the "position of attention." Still I had no feeling. My first thought was what the doctor had told me when I left the hospital first time. The time was approximately 0300 hours when I got on the phone to call the emergency room at Keesler Medical Center in Mississippi. I told them my concerns, and they assured me that I would be okay, and my penis-wenie would be just fine. Just to make sure, I would have to be at Keesler AFB in seven hours. I packed a few necessary items for the trip and a possible extended stay in the hospital. I drove Sandra to her house and headed to Mississippi, holding my penis all the way hoping for some feeling. At 1200 hours, I arrived at the medical center and immediately checked myself into the hospital. That afternoon, the doctors conducted their visits, and I was given a thorough exam and scheduled for more X-rays of my neck. Everything proved to be normal. After three days in the hospital, the feeling started to return to my favorite body part. The stress was gone, and my return trip to Georgia was imminent. I could not wait to use my little soldier at the "position of attention." When I got to my house, Sandra was my first visitor. She was too happy to see an erection with feeling. Sandra and I really enjoyed my homecoming. She even understood the essence of SHIT.

Chapter 17

The End of SHIT

The summer in 1988 was beautiful. I had received my retirement orders which gave me a retirement date of September 1, 1988. I was extremely happy. After all, retiring from the military signifies the end of more than twenty-six years of SHIT. However, that time was well spent in the service of my country. I completed a tour in Vietnam, two tours in Korea, one tour in Germany, and three tours in the Philippines for a total of approximately fifteen years away from home and family. My Stateside assignments include one in Texas and California, two in Florida, two in Kansas, and one in Georgia. I enjoyed all my places I called home. My favorite place was Tampa, Florida, and the Philippines outside the USA.

With orders in hands, it was time to go home to Velma and the boys. However, the USAF threw a monkey wrench into my plans. The USAF served me a new tray of SHIT. Due to my neck surgery, my retirement orders were rescinded on August 15, 1988. Can you imagine me telling Velma on our anniversary, which was the next, day that I wouldn't be coming home in two weeks? My marriage was already in a mess, and now the air force would not let me retire. Due to my surgery, I was given a 50 percent disability. My disability caused my retirement to be a setback until further notice. The air force ordered me to report to Wilford Hall Medical Center at Lackland AFB, Texas. It was a good thing to be compensated for me having been hurt on active duty. It was a bad thing because I had a job waiting for me in Wichita in the field of Equal Employment Opportunity. I was the most qualified with more than ten years' experience and five college degrees of which two were from two local universities (Newman and Wichita State University). My qualifications went from most qualified to not qualified. I became not qualified because the job had a start date of September 1988. I had been extended for medical reasons with a date for retirement unknown. Wilford Hall Medical Center does all the evaluation for medical retirements and discharges. Therefore, I had to be evaluated by the medical staff, the medical evaluation and a medical hearing with lawyers and doctors over a two-week period to determine that I qualify for 50 percent disability.

When I entered the hearing room, the first person I noticed was Col. Dyer. He had been the hospital commander at McConnell AFB, Kansas. Col. Dyer knew me and my physical condition just five years prior. At the age of forty, I was beating his twenty-year-old son in tennis without any sweat. I didn't expect to be the same as I was twenty-five years ago, but I did expect to be where I was just five years ago.

One may ask, "What is a 50 percent disability to a military person with more than twenty-six years of service?" My retirement was secured at twenty years of service. Well, a 50 percent disability allows the IRS to tax only half of my retirement.

This whole retirement process took a total of six months from my original retirement date of September 1, 1988. I was temporarily retired on February 22, 1989. With retirement orders in hand, I decided to do a Didy (Do it yourself) move. I purchased a large van from Richard Appling. Three days later, I loaded my car on a rack and headed for Kansas. The van started acting up when I arrived in Montgomery, Alabama. Thinking I could make it home, I left Montgomery but only got about thirty miles when the van started running hot. I drove to a mechanic shop whereby I was given the bad news that the motor needed new heads. I called Richard and had him send me two Chevy motor heads on the bus. With the cost for the labor on the car and hotel for three days, the majority of the money I had made on the Didy move was almost gone. I called Velma before leaving Alabama, and she informed me that Vincent was very sick. Getting home as soon as possible became a priority. I said a prayer and headed home. The February weather was terrible with Interstate 70 becoming very slick by the minute from heavy snow. I was outside Fort Scott, Arkansas.

I made the decision to not go any further. The van was sliding all over the highway from the snow and wind, not to mention the weight of the contents in the van and hauling my car. I took the first exit and ended up at a farmhouse. Being a black man in rural Arkansas, I was very uncomfortable going up to this isolated house. I presented the little old lady with my military id card and explained my dilemma. She was so understanding that she allowed me to leave the van filled with my household good in her barn. I unloaded my car from the rack and again headed for OZ Land but not before giving the lady my phone number and address in Kansas. The lady wished me good luck and gave me her phone number just in case. Twelve hours later, I arrived in Wichita, Kansas. The family was doing fine with Vince feeling much better. I too felt good to just be home without the pressure of SHIT.

For the next five years, I had to report to Wilford Hall Medical Center for two weeks each year for an annual evaluation to determine whether my condition improved, stayed static, or had gotten worse. Based on their finding, it was determined if the 50 percent disability increased or was reduced. There is always an upside to all situations. The military gave me a two-week all-expense-paid vacation to San Antonio, Texas, for the next four years. After the first four years, the doctors decided my condition was permanent and a fifth year would not be necessary. I was somewhat upset because I would not be getting my two-week vacation the following year. However, I was now fully retired and did not have to worry about any future wars. I could now sing that old hymn "Free at last. Free at last. Thank God Almighty I am Free at Last" from the military serving SHIT. Above all, please remember, SHIT (Servicemen Have It Tough).